Praise for *Designing Workplace Mentoring Programs*:

"*Designing Workplace Mentoring Programs* by Allen, Finkelstein, and Poteet does an excellent job of applying relevant theoretical and empirical research for designing, implementing, and evaluating formal mentor programs. I believe that both academicians and practitioners will enjoy and benefit from reading this book."

Daniel Turban, University of Missouri

"The collective mentoring experiences of leaders from major companies went into this well researched book. Read it first and save yourself a lot of misdirected efforts creating an exemplary program for your organization."

Barry M. Cohen, Ph.D., Consulting Psychologist

"Allen et al. have created a very practical and useful guide to developing workplace mentoring programs. For any HR Professional considering implementing such a program in their organization, this should be their blueprint."

Mariangela Battista, Ph.D., Vice President, Organizational Culture & Effectiveness, Starwood Hotels & Resorts Worldwide, Inc.

"This essential volume offers a practical blueprint for building effective mentoring programs from the ground floor up. Using case interviews, best practices, and existing research, the authors offer a comprehensive guide that is firmly rooted in cutting-edge research. This is a 'must-have' resource for every practitioner's bookshelf."

Belle Rose Ragins, University of Wisconsin-Milwaukee

"If you are planning or currently implementing a mentoring program – this book is a must read. Its clear, concise presentation of research, combined with action plans and case studies takes the guesswork out of program success."

Ann Gowdey, MSW, Principal, Ann Gowdey Consulting

"For the first time, Allen and colleagues have artfully presented a comprehensive, well integrated set of evidence-based recommendations for the design, delivery, and evaluation of formal mentoring programs in organizational settings. This is a must read book for practitioners, who have been heretofore relying primarily on anecdotal evidence to help them create effective mentoring programs, often times with mixed success. The book also has strong appeal to academics because it provides a roadmap for cutting-edge, timely, and important research that can further reduce the science-to-practice gap related to organizational mentoring. The authors should be commended for their ability to take empirical research on formal mentoring programs and create a set of user-friendly guidelines and diagnostic tools to assist in the development of formal mentoring programs. This book is positioned to have a major impact on the field of mentoring and is sure to enhance the mentoring experience for mentors, protégés, and organizations alike."

Lillian T. Eby, Professor of Psychology, University of Georgia

Talent Management Essentials

Series Editor: Steven G. Rogelberg, Ph.D
Professor and Director Organizational Science, University of North Carolina –
Charlotte

Senior Advisory Board:
- Eric Elder, Ph.D., Director, Talent Management, Corning Incorporated
- William H. Macey, Ph.D., Chief Executive Officer, Valtera Corporation
- Cindy McCauley, Ph.D., Senior Fellow, Center for Creative Leadership
- Elaine Pulakos, Ph.D., Chief Operating Officer, Personnel Decisions Research
  Institutes
- Douglas H. Reynolds, Ph.D., Vice President, Assessment Technology,
  Development Dimensions International
- Ann-Marie Ryan, Ph.D., Professor, Michigan State University
- Lise Saari, Ph.D., Direct, Global Workforce Research, IBM
- John Scott, Ph.D., Vice President, Applied Psychological Techniques, Inc.
- Dean Stamoulis, Ph.D., Managing Director, Executive Assessment Practice Leader
  for the Americas, Russell Reynolds Associates

Special Features

Each volume contains a host of actual case studies, sample materials, tips, and
cautionary notes. Issues pertaining to globalization, technology, and key executive
points are highlighted throughout.

Titles in the Talent Management Essentials series:

Performance Management: A New Approach for Driving Business Results
Elaine D. Pulakos

Designing and Implementing Global Selection Systems
Ann-Marie Ryan and Nancy Tippins

Designing Workplace Mentoring Programs: An Evidence-Based Approach
Tammy D. Allen, Lisa M. Finkelstein, and Mark L. Poteet

Career Paths: Charting Courses to Success for Individuals, Organizations, and Industries
Gary W. Carter, Kevin W. Cook and David W. Dorsey

Mistreatment in the Workplace: Prevention and Resolution for Managers and Organizations
Julie B. Olson-Buchanan and Wendy R. Boswell

Developing Women Leaders: A Guide for Men and Women in Organizations
Anna Marie Valerio

Employee Engagement: Tools for Analysis, Practice, and Competitive Advantage
William H. Macey, Benjamin Schneider, Karen M. Barbera, and Scott A. Young

Online Recruiting and Selection: Innovations in Talent Acquisition
Doug Reynolds and John Weiner

Senior Executive Assessment: A Key to Responsible Corporate Governance
Dean Stamoulis

Real-Time Leadership Development
Paul R. Yost and Mary Mannion Plunkett

Designing Workplace Mentoring Programs

An Evidence-Based Approach

Tammy D. Allen, Lisa M. Finkelstein, and Mark L. Poteet

WILEY-BLACKWELL

A John Wiley & Sons, Ltd., Publication

This edition first published 2009
© 2009 Tammy D. Allen, Lisa M. Finkelstein, and Mark L. Poteet

Blackwell Publishing was acquired by John Wiley & Sons in February 2007. Blackwell's publishing program has been merged with Wiley's global Scientific, Technical, and Medical business to form Wiley-Blackwell.

Registered Office
John Wiley & Sons Ltd, The Atrium, Southern Gate, Chichester, West Sussex, PO19 8SQ, United Kingdom

Editorial Offices
350 Main Street, Malden, MA 02148-5020, USA
9600 Garsington Road, Oxford, OX4 2DQ, UK
The Atrium, Southern Gate, Chichester, West Sussex, PO19 8SQ, UK

For details of our global editorial offices, for customer services, and for information about how to apply for permission to reuse the copyright material in this book please see our website at www.wiley.com/wiley-blackwell.

The right of Tammy D. Allen, Lisa M. Finkelstein, and Mark L. Poteet to be identified as the authors of this work has been asserted in accordance with the Copyright, Designs and Patents Act 1988.

Wiley also publishes its books in a variety of electronic formats. Some content that appears in print may not be available in electronic books.

Designations used by companies to distinguish their products are often claimed as trademarks. All brand names and product names used in this book are trade names, service marks, trademarks or registered trademarks of their respective owners. The publisher is not associated with any product or vendor mentioned in this book. This publication is designed to provide accurate and authoritative information in regard to the subject matter covered. It is sold on the understanding that the publisher is not engaged in rendering professional services. If professional advice or other expert assistance is required, the services of a competent professional should be sought.

Library of Congress Cataloging-in-Publication Data

Allen, Tammy D.
    Designing workplace mentoring programs : an evidence-based approach / Tammy D. Allen, Lisa M. Finkelstein, and Mark L. Poteet.
        p. cm. – (Talent management essentials)
    Includes bibliographical references and index.
    ISBN 978-1-4051-7989-8 (hardcover : alk. paper) – ISBN 978-1-4051-7990-4 (pbk. : alk. paper)
1. Mentoring in business.   2. Mentoring in business–Case studies.   I. Finkelstein, Lisa M.
II. Poteet, Mark L.   III. Title.
    HF5385.A55   2009
    658.3′124–dc22

                                                                                    2008044059

A catalogue record for this book is available from the British Library.

Icon in Case Scenario boxes © Kathy Konkle/istockphoto.com

Set in 10.5 on 12.5pt Minion by SNP Best-set Typesetter Ltd., Hong Kong

1   2009

Contents

Series Editor's Preface

The *Talent Management Essentials* series presents state-of-the-art thinking on critical talent management topics ranging from global staffing, to career pathing, to engagement, to executive staffing, to performance management, to mentoring, to real-time leadership development. Authored by leading authorities and scholars on their respective topics, each volume offers state-of-the-art thinking and the epitome of evidence-based practice. These authors bring to their books an incredible wealth of experience working with small, large, public and private organizations, as well as keen insights into the science and best practices associated with talent management.

Written succinctly and without superfluous "fluff," this series provides powerful and practical treatments of essential talent topics critical to maximizing individual and organizational health, well-being and effectiveness. The books, taken together, provide a comprehensive and contemporary treatment of approaches, tools, and techniques associated with Talent Management. The goal of the series is to produce focused, prescriptive volumes that translate the data- and practice-based knowledge of I/O psychology and Organizational Behavior into practical, "how to" advice for dealing with cutting-edge organizational issues and problems.

Talent Management Essentials is a comprehensive, practitioner-oriented series of "best practices" for the busy solution-oriented manager, executive, HR leader, and consultant. And, in its application of evidence-based practice, this series will also appeal to professors, executive MBA students, and graduate students in Organizational Behavior, Human Resources Management, and I/O Psychology.

Preface

In recent years, formal mentoring programs have become increasingly recognized as an organizational best practice. Mentoring programs help organizations develop leaders, retain diverse and skilled employees, and enhance succession planning. Executed properly, such programs can be used to give organizations a competitive edge in the escalating "war for talent." However, as scientists-practitioners who have been conducting research and working with organizations on employee development issues for many years, we have been painfully aware that there has been little in the way of evidenced-based guidance to organizations with regard to developing formal mentoring programs. This book is designed to fill this gap.

Individuals looking for a "one-size-fits-all" guide to formal mentoring programs may be disappointed with our efforts. We took the approach that organizations are best served by having a clear understanding of the various issues that should be taken into consideration when designing and executing a formal mentoring program. It is our ultimate goal to give organizations the information they need to build a customized mentoring program that meets each organization's unique needs. We provide tools that we believe will be useful toward that end and we share examples from organizations experienced in running successful programs. Readers of the book will come away with an actionable guide and plan for the development of programs that can be tailored to their own organization.

Two overarching themes are repeated throughout the book. One theme is that organizations should develop the program with specific objectives in mind and to base decisions regarding the design and structure of the program on those objectives. The mentoring program should be strategically aligned with the organization's core values and mission. This is a simple message applicable to practically any organizational intervention. The second theme is that organizations should keep in mind that, at its core, mentoring involves an interpersonal relationship. This is the essence of what makes a formal mentoring program unique from, but potentially more powerful than, many other organizational programs and, ironically, what makes a formal mentoring program difficult to implement successfully. Accordingly, decisions regarding design features and structure should be made with the thought of facilitating effective relational processes.

Our recommendations are based on the context of a one-on-one relationship in which the mentor is the senior employee and the protégé is the more junior employee. There are other less common formats that formal mentoring programs may take that include peer mentoring, group mentoring, upward mentoring, or a combination of these. We believe there are benefits to these types of programs. For example, the argument has been made that by having a protégé interact with more than one mentor (and vice versa), the importance of (and problems with) "interpersonal chemistry" can be lessened, and the protégé also has the benefit of being exposed to multiple viewpoints. Upward mentoring programs, in which junior employees take the role of the mentor and members of upper management are the protégés, can be an effective way of bringing new knowledge and expanded awareness to senior leadership within the organization. However, research on these alternative forms of mentoring is extremely scarce. Because the majority of formal mentoring programs and research continues to focus on one-on-one relationships, our guidelines also reflect that mentoring format.

There are some distinct terms used in the book that we want to define for readers. A *meta-analysis* is a statistical method that combines the results of multiple independent research studies that examine a single research question of interest. When the results of a meta-analysis are reported, this indicates that the data, results, and conclusions presented are based on a combination of multiple studies rather than a single research effort. Understandably, this leads to more reliable and valid conclusions. Although we do not advocate that any one term is better than the other, we have elected to use the term *protégé* when referring to the targeted learner within the formal mentoring program. In other books and within many organizations, including those we interviewed, the term "mentee" or "mentoree" may be considered acceptable and used instead of "protégé."

Features of This Book

When we began planning this book, we knew we wanted to interview people who manage mentoring programs in order to provide readers with an "on-the-ground" sense of what is really happening within the day-to-day operations of a program, what is working, and what is not, in order to bring to life our research-based recommendations. We designed a semi-structured interview that followed the format of the book, tracing a mentoring program from its initial inception through planning, support, goal setting, matching, training, monitoring, and evaluation. We conducted interviews by phone. Some of the questions included:

- What are the goals for the program?
- How is support for the program demonstrated to participants?
- What characteristics are used in making matches?
- Are there any components of the training that you think have been particularly useful or effective for the pair to hit the ground running?
- Have you tried anything in the course of the program that did not work out the way it was intended?

Our sample of companies included in these interviews was not random. We relied on our professional contacts and personal knowledge of companies with programs that we admired. We were only able to talk with those who wanted to talk about mentoring. However, we were delighted that a wide variety of individuals, who represented a variety of industries and types of mentoring programs, were willing to share their time and their stories, providing a unique window into operational mentoring programs. Information gleaned from these interviews can be found throughout the book featured in "Case

Study" and "Lessons Learned" boxes. Additionally, in "Case Study Summary" boxes, we highlight common themes that cut across multiple companies. With regard to the organizations interviewed, we respected their request to be identified by name or to remain anonymous. Accordingly, throughout the book the reader will note information sometimes references specific companies and sometimes references companies by industry.

Other notable features of the book include an assortment of tools, forms, questionnaires, and exercises that can be readily copied or modified for organizational use. To make it easy for the reader to locate, these features are included at the end of the book as a set of Appendices. "Good to Know" boxes that include summary points related to research findings are found throughout the book. Additionally, at the end of most chapters, we provide a step-by-step action plan as an implementation guide to the points covered in the chapter.

We are excited to meld our collective knowledge of the empirical research on mentoring with common practices within organizations in the attempt to guide organizations toward the successful development and implementation of formal mentoring programs. Additional collaborations between organizations and researchers are needed to continue to hone what we know and to enable the dissemination of evidence-based knowledge of effective mentoring practices for all stakeholders. It is our hope and our intent that this book will help organizations harness the power of mentoring in a way that benefits both individuals and organizations.

Chapter 1

Introduction

As the number of organizations implementing workplace formal mentoring programs continues to grow, such programs can no longer be considered but one more passing fad. The proliferation of formal mentoring efforts is no surprise, given the vast array of benefits that have been associated with mentoring. Mentoring relationships are thought to serve a critical role in an employee's career and skill development, key to retaining top talent, and a fundamental way by which organizations can shape corporate leadership. Given the continuing need for companies to groom early-career employees for succession planning purposes, to facilitate the upward mobility of under-represented groups, and to respond to organizational structural changes, there is reason to believe that the use of such programs will continue to flourish. However, the implementation of these programs should be done with care in that a poorly designed and executed formal mentoring program may do more harm than good.

Until recently, there has been very little empirical research to help guide the development of workplace mentoring programs. The aim of the current volume is to provide guidelines based on a synthesis of empirical research so that formal mentoring programs can achieve their full potential as a significant employee development tool. The recommendations made throughout the book are based on the existing research evidence and supplemented by examples based on interviews conducted with organizations that have formal mentoring programs in place.

Defining Mentoring

Workplace mentoring is traditionally described as a relationship between two individuals, usually a senior and junior employee, whereby the senior employee takes the junior employee "under his or her wing" to teach the junior employee about his or her job, introduce the junior employee to contacts, orient the employee to the industry and organization, and address social and personal issues that may arise on the job. Mentoring can also be defined by the behaviors that comprise the relationship. Specifically, mentors are thought to provide two primary forms of support to their protégés.[1] *Career-related support* focuses on protégé success and advancement within the organization, and includes exposure and visibility, coaching, protection, sponsorship, and challenging assignments. *Psychosocial support* centers on the enhancement of the protégé's sense of identity, competence, and effectiveness as a professional, and includes friendship, acceptance and confirmation, counseling, and role modeling. Research generally shows that the more that mentors demonstrate these behaviors to their protégés (e.g., the more opportunities they offer the protégé to be exposed to other key figures in the organization; the more counseling they provide to the protégé), the more positive the outcomes of the relationship.[2]

There are several defining characteristics that set mentoring apart from other workplace relationships.[3] First, mentoring is a two-person relationship between a more experienced person (a mentor) and a less experienced person (a protégé). Second, the relationship is one of mutuality, yet it also asymmetrical. Both the mentor and the protégé may benefit from the relationship, but the primary focus is the growth and development of the protégé. Third, mentoring relationships are dynamic. The relational processes and outcomes associated with mentoring change over time. The mentoring relationship often differs from the typical supervisor–subordinate relationship in the following features:

- The mentor and protégé do not have to necessarily work together.

- The mentor usually does not have any formal or reward power over the protégé.
- The mentor may be several levels higher in the organization and in a different line of responsibility than the protégé.

The terms "mentoring" and "coaching" are often used interchangeably. Indeed, there are several similarities between the two forms of employee development. For example, both can be done over an extended period of time, and both can include developmental activities such as giving constructive feedback, teaching the protégé/coachee a new behavior or approach, and goal setting and action planning. However, there are some key differences between the two terms:

- Coaching is often more instruction-focused – typically the focus is on specific tasks or specific skills that the employee currently needs or will need in order to perform his or her work effectively.
- Because it is more skill and knowledge-based, coaching is often provided by professionals who are external to the organization and who, in theory, can work with the coachee objectively and confidentially (e.g., professional consultants).
- Coaching interventions are often based on careful diagnosis of the coachee's specific needs, frequently using observation, interviews, and skill assessment tools.
- Mentoring often addresses or focuses on issues that are broader than those covered in the typical coaching relationship, such as sponsorship, introduction to key figures, increasing the protégé's contacts, orienting a new employee to the organization, and helping the protégé learn about the organization's unwritten rules. Anything done to help the employee's orientation, career, and professional development can be included under the broad term of mentoring.
- Because mentoring is broader in its focus, it can and often does include aspects of teaching and skill-based instruction. Therefore, coaching is a tool that can be used within a mentoring relationship.
- Because mentoring activities are often focused on issues specific to the context of the organization (e.g., broadening a protégé's network within the company; helping the protégé learn the company's politics; sponsoring the protégé for promotional opportunities),

mentoring is most often done by an internal, more senior member of the company (rather than an external consultant).

A *formal* mentoring program – the focus of this volume – is one in which the organization plays an intervening role in facilitating employee mentoring relationships by providing some level of structure, guidelines, policies, and assistance for starting, maintaining, and ending mentor–protégé relationships. As will be discussed throughout the book, the nature of the organization's role at each of these stages will not look exactly the same across all organizations. Organizationally sanctioned mentoring relationships are different from those that naturally occur within the organization. In naturally occurring mentoring relationships, it is the mentor and/or the protégé who initiate, maintain, and end a relationship, with little or no official organizational support.

Why Do Mentoring?

The primary reason to facilitate mentoring relationships is that they have been associated with a variety of widely publicized organizational, as well as individual, benefits. The popular press is replete with articles carrying titles such as, "The power of mentoring: finding the right advisor can give your career a boost," "A mentor is a key to career success," and "Find yourself a mentor." It is also not uncommon for well-known business leaders to attribute their success to having a mentor.[4] The guidance of a mentor can be a critical resource to individuals early in their career, while serving as a mentor to others during the later career years can provide a sense of accomplishment. The benefits of mentoring have been well established within the academic literature as well, with meta-analytic research supporting positive career benefits for protégés who have been mentored within a formal mentoring program.[5] However, as we noted earlier, poorly designed and executed mentoring programs can be damaging to the organization and its members. Moreover, a formal mentoring program may not be right for every organization or a program may be implemented for the wrong reason. This book is designed to help determine if mentoring is right for your organization and, if so, provide guidance as to how to most effectively structure the program.

Good to Know:
Outcomes Associated with Mentoring[6]

For the Protégé:

- Higher compensation and faster salary growth
- More promotions and higher expectations for advancement
- Higher job and career satisfaction
- Greater career and organizational commitment

For the Mentor:

- Enhanced career success
- Career revitalization
- Personal growth and satisfaction

For the Organization:

- Enhanced organizational attraction and recruitment
- Reduced employee turnover
- Increased organizational learning and employee socialization

---

Goal of This Book

The main objective of this book is to present an evidence-based best practice approach to the design, development, and operation of formal mentoring programs within organizations. We will inform the reader as to what research tells us about effective formal mentoring practices. A "start-to-finish" guide is provided that can be used by management, employee development professionals, and formal mentoring program administrators. The design of formal mentoring programs can vary considerably. Some programs are highly structured while others take a more casual approach. Research shows that programs with a greater degree of organizational facilitation and structure are generally more effective than those with little support and oversight.[7] Importantly, organizations should consider the cumulative effect of implementing multiple "best practice" features into their program. The impact of any one practice alone may be minimal.[8] Notably, facilitation and structure should not be equated with rigidity and inflexible formality. The form that the facilitation and structure takes needs to fit with the culture of the organization.

The recommendations found in this book are based on the academic, empirical research literature that has examined effective formal mentoring practices, data from companies that have implemented formal programs, and case studies of formal mentoring programs in organizations. However, we also recognize that there is much that we do not know yet regarding formal mentoring program design and effectiveness. We do not pull any punches – if the research evidence is not there, we tell you. In those cases, factors to take into consideration based on other research literature are offered. We also profile some of the obstacles and barriers that organizations reported facing in the execution of their programs. We believe that with the anticipation of potential pitfalls, companies can develop sound risk mitigation and back-up strategies to ensure that their programs do not derail. As an initial overview to the mentoring process we present the first of our case studies. The cases below each illustrate the general approaches to formal mentoring taken by Starwood Hotels and by KPMG.

Case Study:
Starwood Hotels

Starwood Hotels & Resorts Worldwide, Inc. is a leading international hospitality company with over 870 properties managed in over 95 countries under several brand names (St. Regis®, The Luxury Collection®, W®, Westin®, Le Méridien®, Sheraton®, Four Points® by Sheraton, Aloft(SM), and Element(SM)), employing over 150,000 associates. Its mentoring program, referred to as the mentor network, is centered on a web-based tool that provides associates worldwide a common framework to help them create mentoring relationships. This framework focuses on helping mentors and protégés to define goals, determine which of Starwood Hotels' leadership competencies are to be developed, and to measure progress. The program was created in response to associates asking for mentoring programs in Starwood Hotels' annual engagement survey, as well as the company's need to provide structure and guidance to mentoring programs that were being implemented at local sites. The overall goal of the mentor network is to provide coaching and development opportunities for associates to help prepare them for potential leadership roles in the future. Although the mentor network is still in its early phases of implementation, several key features stand out:

- First, support for the program was demonstrated at multiple levels in the organization – from top management through Executive Level participation on a taskforce to help define the program, and from local general managers who champion the program by attending the local, on-site kickoffs.
- Second, the program allows for much flexibility and ownership at the "local property level." For example, local property management has significant input and decision-making responsibility for who participates as mentors and protégés, as well as how mentors and protégés are matched. Also, while suggestions are offered from the mentor network program owners, local management determines various aspects of the relationship's structure (e.g., frequency of meetings, duration of relationship, activities to be undertaken).
- At the same time, by providing a common process and corporate-level support, the purpose and expectations for each local mentoring program are much more clear, specific, and understandable. According to Corinne Donovan from Starwood Hotels' Organizational Culture & Effectiveness group, this helps prevent properties from "creating a mentoring program just for the sake of having one."
- Fourth, the mentor network provides comprehensive orientation and training to help mentoring relationships get started. Using some combination of live, or web-conference-based delivery, mentors and protégés are briefed on different learning styles, each participant's role, mentoring concepts, and how to prepare for the developmental relationship. Protégés receive further assistance with setting goals and expectations for the relationship.
- Fifth, after the six-month time period, Starwood Hotels administers a survey to evaluate the success of the overall program as well as each mentoring relationship, looking at issues such as trust, learning that has taken place, what mentors have benefited from, and whether protégés have been challenged.

According to Corinne Donovan, Manager, Organizational Culture & Effectiveness group and Mariangela Battista, Vice President, Organizational Culture & Effectiveness group, feedback from surveys, as well as anecdotal informal feedback, has been positive. Protégés have learned about themselves, gotten more exposure in the organization, and are in a better position to take on individual responsibilities. Also, many mentors have broadened their perspectives and learned from the experience as well. Finally, both mentors and protégés who report having good quality mentoring relationships are more likely to remain with Starwood Hotels.

Case Study:
KPMG LLP

KPMG LLP, a member of KPMG International, is a Big Four Audit, Tax, and Advisory firm with over 1,800 partners and 23,000 employees located across 93 offices in the United States. Although mentoring had been occurring informally for years, KPMG's Chairman and Deputy Chairman at the time, realizing mentoring's value in their own careers, began a push to formalize the process. Also, at the time, internal employee survey results indicated that a substantial majority of associates were interested in either finding or being a mentor. The overall goals of the program were to increase employees' connection with the firm and their development in order that they would progress and remain at KPMG throughout their careers. KPMG makes its mentoring program available to all employees, regardless of level or career track. Other unique features include the following:

- There are many incentives for people to participate as mentors. First, "serving as a mentor" is sometimes included on goal-setting forms as part of the performance review process. Second, KPMG has created a "National Mentoring Award" to reward and recognize top mentors at a dinner with the senior management. Third, on National Mentoring Day, all mentors nominated for the National Mentoring Award are sent an electronic "thank you" letter containing feedback from their protégé(s).
- Comprehensive training is offered for both mentors and protégés. Common topics are presented, such as defining roles and expectations for each participant; specialized topics are also covered in separate training modules for mentors (e.g., how to provide constructive feedback) and protégés (e.g., learning quickly). As employees are very dispersed and are often in client meetings, training is delivered via an interactive Internet web-cast. Training is offered many times, and recorded playback of the web-casts is available. Employees often leave training learning that mentoring should be goal-focused and not necessarily a lifelong relationship.
- KPMG evaluates the success of its mentoring efforts through an annual employee survey as well as through retention statistics. According to Barbara Wankoff, National Director of Workplace Solutions, and Steven Katzman, Associate Director of Organizational Effectiveness, over 9,500 mentoring relationships have occurred, covering 15,000 employees. Survey scores regarding

mentoring and career growth satisfaction are positive, and across all classification levels (i.e., staff, management, partners), those employees with mentors demonstrate significantly less turnover than those without, resulting in an estimated cost savings of $33m.

Organization of the Book

The organization of the book is such that the chapters follow roughly the same order as the steps taken to develop a formal program. In Chapter 2, we discuss issues related to initial planning and infrastructure. Chapter 3 reviews the topic of recruiting and selecting program participants. Chapter 4 covers matching mentors and protégés. Training is the focus of Chapter 5. Chapter 6 describes mentoring structure and processes while the book closes with the topic of program monitoring and evaluation in Chapter 7. Appendix A consists of a complete list of planning questions that can serve as a framework for overall preparation and development of the program. This planning form is to be used in conjunction with each of the remaining chapters.

Chapter 2

Planning and Providing Infrastructure

As with any organizational intervention, the effectiveness of a formal mentoring program is dependent on adequate planning and infrastructure. Although there are numerous benefits associated with having a formal mentoring program, developing and maintaining the program involves an investment of time, people, effort, and money. The organization must have the infrastructure in place, or create the infrastructure, that fosters the development of high quality mentoring relationships.

When considering whether a formal mentoring program is right for your organization, there are a number of important questions that need to be answered. For example, do you have the organizational capacity to plan and operate an effective program? How will a mentoring program add to existing employee development processes within the organization? Do you have the necessary support from top management? What are the business needs that can be addressed by mentoring? In this chapter we map out the initial steps required to plan the program. The five main issues that are considered include: (1) needs assessment; (2) organizational support for the program; (3) setting program objectives; (4) integration with other Human Resources development strategies and organizational culture; and (5) program administration.

Needs Assessment

The first step to the implementation of a formal mentoring program should be a thorough needs assessment to determine whether a formal mentoring program is required and what needs it will address. Needs assessment is a systematic examination of the way things are, and the way things should be, within the organization. It involves analyzing the current state of the organization as well as the desired state.[1] Needs assessment plays a critical role in the initial planning of any organizational intervention, including a formal mentoring program. The purpose and importance of needs assessment are outlined below.

Purpose and Importance of Needs Assessment

- Provides information to customize the program to meet organizational needs
- Justifies investments in the program – helps make the business case
- Provides criteria for measuring success
- Determines cost effectiveness
- Provides information for program design/redesign
- Increases the probability of success because it determines if and how the program can truly address the identified need
- Provides information regarding how to align the program with overall corporate strategy and other talent management initiatives

When conducting a needs assessment for the purpose of formal mentoring, two levels of analysis are required. Analysis should be conducted at the organizational level and at the person level. An organizational analysis involves an examination of system-wide components of the organization that may impact the mentoring program. It is important to remember that the mentoring program is embedded within a larger organizational system. The organizational analysis involves determining if a mentoring program is appropriate, given the organization's business strategy, the resources available (both tangible and intangible) that can be invested in the program, and support for the program by organizational members. Thus, formation of the mentoring program begins with a review of the organization's long-term, strategic goals, and objectives. A successful mentoring program is one that is purposefully aligned with the organization's overall mission. Specifically, the direction of the mentoring program, as well as its specific components, should be integrated with the organization's overall mission, vision, values, and philosophy.

The person analysis involves identifying who will be the participants of the formal mentoring program and the readiness among organizational members for participation in a mentoring relationship. At the person level, thought should be given not only to who the protégés will be in the program, but also as to who will be the mentors. Mentoring programs must meet the needs and expectations of both protégés and mentors.

Key Issues to Address in the Needs Assessment

Organizational Analysis

- Is mentoring needed to achieve our business objectives?
- How will mentoring support our business strategy?
- Are there problems in the organization that might be solved by mentoring?
- Do we want to spend money and time on formal mentoring?
- What resources do we have available to devote to formal mentoring?
- Will top management support the program? How?
- Are there environmental constraints to the successful implementation of a program?
- What are the expectations for the program?
- Can the program be integrated and aligned with other business and employee development strategies that exist within the organization?
- Can we develop and run the program ourselves or will we need external assistance?
- What are the consequences if we do not implement a formal mentoring program?

Person Analysis

- Who could benefit from mentoring?
- Who is our target group for mentoring?

Continued

- Who could serve as mentors?
- How will we identify participants in the program?
- Are individuals ready and willing to assume the roles of protégés and of mentors?
- What will be the characteristics of program participants?
- What gaps exist in people's willingness and readiness to serve as a protégé or mentor?
- Are we prepared to address those gaps?

A variety of methods can be used to conduct the needs assessment. For example, individual and/or group interviews may be conducted with key stakeholders in the proposed program. Key stakeholders may include those anticipated to participate as mentors and as protégés. Questionnaires may be developed and data collected from employees to determine interest and readiness to participate in a formal program. A review of existing organizational data such as climate survey results, employee opinion surveys, exit interview material, and turnover rates may also be informative. Needs assessment works best when multiple sources of information and multiple viewpoints are included. Reliance on any one source of data may result in an incomplete understanding of needs.

Appendix B presents a list of questions that may be used in an interview or focus group format for the purpose of a needs assessment prior to the development of a formal mentoring program. These questions drill deeper, expanding beyond organizational and person analysis to center on three areas: (1) assessment of the organization; (2) assessment of program design; and (3) assessment of resources. See also the questions posed in Appendix A.

During the needs assessment process, some external scanning of the environment can also help chart the course of action to be taken by the organization. Environmental scanning involves obtaining information about the world outside the organization that can impact decisions made within the organization. Done for the purpose of a mentoring program, this can include collecting information regarding the experiences of similar organizations in implementing formal mentoring programs, the external sources available to help with the design and execution of programs, and human resource trends that may have a bearing on employee development.

Organizational Support for the Program

The organization must show a high level of support in order for a formal mentoring program to succeed. Organizational support is important because employees will be more committed to the program if they believe their leaders value it or, even better, if they see their leaders practice it. It is important for participants to *perceive* this support. That is, in terms of employee reactions to the program, the support needs to be apparent to others within the organization. As perception is key, it is important that organizational support be visible and genuine. Here are some ways that an organization can demonstrate support for the mentoring program:

- Have a communication and marketing plan for the program.
- Include top management as part of the mentoring design and administration team.
- Have top leaders participate as mentors.
- Encourage leaders to publicize the program.
- Have managers express support and provide needed time to subordinates serving as protégés and/or mentors.
- Allow time away from the job for mentors and protégés to meet.
- Hold semi-annual meetings as a way of publicizing the mentoring programs.
- Implement reward systems as a way to encourage mentors to participate.
- Make the formal mentoring program part of a company's overall employee/management development initiative.
- Create a philosophy statement around the mentoring program that links to the mission statement of the organization.
- Utilize the company's website to explain and support the program.

Lessons Learned:
Waning Management Support

Sometimes upper-level management is not behind an initiative, and sometimes the enthusiasm just wanes over time. A representative from one large corporation told us that initially the CEO

Continued

loved the idea of a mentoring program and actively championed the pilot. However, eventually his attention turned to other things. When this happened, there was no longer enthusiasm and commitment among the top management team to serve as mentors, and the program – though still working – has lost some steam and some valuable resources.

In another instance, the CEO who championed a formal mentoring initiative left the company, whereupon the program lost momentum and support. Under the former CEO it had been mandatory for executives to serve as mentors. In the revised program, it is no longer required, but highly encouraged.

Perceived support is critical for multiple reasons. A substantial body of research demonstrates the breadth of the importance of perceived organizational support.[2] Fair treatment (e.g., procedural justice), supervisor support (i.e., employees' achievements are valued; employees' well-being is considered), and rewards and favorable job conditions (e.g., role clarity, job security) are related to perceived organizational support. Perceived support is also associated with positive job attitudes including desire to remain within the organization. Additionally, top management support has been positively related to training adoption and perceived success.[3] For example, top management support for employee assistance programs can influence employees' confidence in the program, leading to increase usage of the program.[4]

Given how strongly organizational support is related to general work outcomes, it can be reasonably inferred that organizational support for a mentoring program may result in increased commitment to and intention to use the program. For example, it has been found that by promoting a culture that models positive behavior, organizational support can play a key role in preventing negative mentoring behaviors.[5] Other research has shown that support from one's immediate workgroup can also enhance the mentoring process.[6] Finally, mentors who perceive that management is supportive of the formal mentoring program also find the formal mentoring experience more rewarding.[7] When mentors perceive that management support is lacking, they also report the concern that if their protégés fail, it will reflect badly on them. Such perceptions can result in a decreased willingness to be a formal mentor.

Lessons Learned

- The fact that senior executives who sponsor the program also mentor multiple protégés each sends a strong message about top management commitment.
- When executives are visible at key events, like the mentoring kick-off or an award ceremony, it shows they view mentoring as a top priority.
- When a company has operations in many locations, having local champions may matter even more than having just top management support; "top management" is not always visible to employees, but local management is.

Setting Program Objectives

The needs assessment process should result in the establishment of objectives and intended outcomes. The objectives will influence decisions about the structure of the program, such as who should participate and under what conditions. Mentoring programs can be designed for a variety of organizational objectives. For example, in a study of 127 formal mentoring programs across industries, the developmental objectives most often cited were managerial talent development (42%), skill building (33%), diversity development (24%), and new employee socialization (21%).[8] There is no evidence that the overall effectiveness of a formal mentoring program differs depending on its objective, but it has been suggested that more specific and targeted objectives lead to superior outcomes than do vague or overly broad objectives.[9] It should be kept in mind that the purpose of the program will likely impact various outcomes differently. For example, programs aimed at new employee socialization may increase employee knowledge of the organization but have little impact on satisfaction with promotion opportunities. We return this issue when we discuss program evaluation in Chapter 7. Note also that a program may be designed to meet multiple needs and that the objectives listed above are not mutually exclusive. What is clear is that organizations need to establish objectives for the program, objectives need to be based on organizational needs, and objectives need to be clearly communicated to all employees. Research shows that both mentors and protégés strongly recommend that organizations clarify program objectives as a means of improving formal relationships.[10]

Case Study Summary

One company noted that since integrating their informal programs under a common framework and purpose, individual roles have been clarified, expectations are more specific and understandable, and the program has been running more smoothly. In fact, the company will not create a mentoring process for a local organization unless it is clear about the purpose and expectations of the proposed process. Other companies noted that letting participants know what mentoring is and is not, and what will and will not be outcomes of participation, was important for grounding participants' expectations and giving them a framework to facilitate an effective relationship.

While establishing objectives of the program, markers of program success should also be identified to enable program evaluation at a later date. What outcomes are you trying to achieve? How will you know if the program is successful or not? The outcomes identified should be specific, measurable, realistic and achievable aims that are aligned with the company's strategy and tailored to program objectives and the target group to be mentored. For example, a vague goal such as "increase retention" can be made more specific by restating along the lines of, "increase retention of women in the organization by 20%." Organizations should carefully consider and clearly delineate how it is that mentoring will help achieve these goals (e.g., "How can the program be designed in order to increase retention of women by 20%?").

Some thinking at this point regarding monitoring and evaluation of the program (see Chapter 7) is also necessary for planning purposes. For example, the organization should consider the processes and steps it will put in place to deal with mentoring relationships that are encountering difficulties but can be repaired, versus those relationships that are irrevocably damaged and or ineffective, and should be terminated.

Good to Know:
Common Purposes of Formal Mentoring Programs

- Leadership development
- Identification of high potential employees
- Retention of diverse, highly skilled and talented employees

- Support mechanism for new and/or diverse employees
- Provide access to company leaders
- Succession planning
- Employee skill development

Integration with Other HR Systems and Processes

As noted above, the mentoring program should be consonant with an overall corporate strategy, but as a human resource (HR) development strategy, it should also harmonize with other organizational employee development and talent management efforts. The four primary functions of human resource development that formal mentoring most clearly is linked to are organization development, training and development, succession planning, and career development.[11] Mentoring can be part of a planned changed effort, a form of employee job training, and a career development mechanism. The mentoring program should be in partnership with these other functions within the organization. For example, a company interested in succession planning for future executive leadership vacancies can use formal mentoring as but one component of the overall talent development program, in conjunction with other developmental activities such as job rotations, shadow committees, and special project work. In this case it can be stressed that mentoring is not *the* intervention, but is *an* intervention.

Case Study Summary

Many companies stated that embedding formal mentoring within other existing programs was an important factor to program success. For example, one company noted that including the formal mentoring process within a broader framework of existing

Continued

leadership development activities was a way to help people see its relevance and contribution to their growth and success. Another company included formal mentoring as one building block within its overall "career architecture." Another company noted that linking mentor participation to the performance management program is effective in ensuring participation. Other companies tie their formal mentoring programs into broader diversity initiatives as a way of increasing opportunities for female and minority employees. Another company recommends participation in formal mentoring as a factor to be considered in promotion decisions.

Some thinking should also go into how mentoring fits within the overall culture and structure of the organization. While we believe best practices exist based on research evidence, it is still possible that a program model that is successful in one organization will be a failure in another. For example, a mentoring program may be ineffective if it is highly rigid, rule-driven, and structured when the organization itself is based on a flexible and autonomous work environment. In general, any formal mentoring program will have difficulty succeeding if the overall climate of the organization does not place a high value on employee learning and development. Research indicates that formal mentoring may be more likely to flourish in organizations that place an emphasis on teamwork, collaboration, and open communication.[12]

Lessons Learned

- Ensure that the program is integrated into other employee development programs.
- Develop or modify the mentoring program to fit the organization's unique culture.
- Do not expect mentoring to be a "silver bullet," but to be one piece of the overall talent management puzzle.

Program Administration

It is important that someone is identified as associated with administrating and managing the central functions of the mentoring program. Often referred to as the Program Administrator, this person may be embedded within other units such as Human Resources, employee training and development, diversity, etc. Sample responsibilities that program administrators execute include:

- Provide oversight of the mentoring program
- Communicate as needed with program stakeholders
- Obtain and maintain support from senior management
- Recommend mentor and protégé matches
- Be available to mentors and protégés to address problems and provide resources
- Provide oversight of program-related training
- Conduct program evaluation
- Report program results
- Monitor and revise program structure as needed

In carrying out these activities, the program administrator may work with a steering committee or advisory board that provides input and guidance. Ideally the steering committee includes executives. Including executives serves the purpose of demonstrating that the program has high-level support and that the program stays synchronized with the strategic goals of the organization. The steering committee may also include organizational members who can represent those who the program is designed to serve. This helps ensure that the program meets the needs of the intended targets. Finally, the steering committee may also benefit from including representatives who cut across various organizational functions to help ensure a variety of viewpoints are recognized. As an example, one of the companies that we interviewed has an executive steering committee, consisting of the program's sponsor and several other senior leaders, that meets quarterly to discuss how well the mentoring program and relationships are functioning, to investigate any problems, and to provide solutions to the issues identified. The committee also receives periodic feedback on challenges and experiences from mentors and provides assistance to them as needed. At another company, each of the executive mentoring committee members also serves as mentors in the program.

Lessons Learned

- Ensure the proper internal and external resources are devoted to the administration and support of the program.

Continued

- Find a good administrative person upfront who will devote the time and energy to watching over the details and running the program.

Action Plan:
Planning and Providing Infrastructure

- Determine the relevant questions to be addressed in a needs assessment (including organizational and person analysis).
- Determine the methods to be used for conducting the needs analysis.
- Determine the stakeholders to participate in the needs analysis.
- Conduct the needs analysis.
- Conduct external scan of the environment.
- Based on the results of the needs assessment, decide whether a formal mentoring program is appropriate. If so, proceed below.
- Determine whether there is an adequate level of upper management and front line support for the program.
- Determine specifically how this support will be behaviorally demonstrated to potential participants.
- Based on the results of the needs assessment, clearly state (in writing) the specific objectives of the program.
- State the specific, measurable outcomes that you would like to achieve.
- Develop a program evaluation plan.
- Review current HR systems and leadership development strategies and determine how mentoring fits into the HR strategy.
- Determine the level of structure and formality that will best fit the organization's culture.
- Select a program administrator, ensuring he or she has the motivation and time for the position.
- Decide if there will be a steering committee, determine the types of people to be represented on the committee, and recruit committee members.
- Determine the specific responsibilities of the program administrator and members of the steering committee, and determine how often they will meet.
- Set a date and an agenda for the initial steering committee meeting.

Chapter 3

Participant Recruitment and Selection

Who should participate as protégés and as mentors in the mentoring program? Should participation be required? Should potential protégés be restricted to certain groups of employees? How will potential mentors be persuaded to devote their time and energy to the mentoring relationships? How will we select and recruit potential mentors and protégés?

One of the first steps in designing a mentoring program is to determine who will participate in the program as protégés and as mentors. In determining who the targeted participants should be, designers of formal mentoring programs should first look to the program's objectives. For example, a program designed to increase the management succession pool of minority employees may logically restrict protégé participation to minority employees.

Because there are often more potential protégé participants than can be accommodated at any one time, typically selection criteria and a decision-making process are needed. Once the typical protégé profile is identified, the recruitment and selection of mentors flow from there. In addition, there are times when the organization may believe that participation in the mentoring program should be required. These are all important factors for consideration. In this chapter, we discuss four issues: (1) general participation guidelines; (2) protégé selection; (3) mentor recruitment; and (4) mentor selection.

General Participation Guidelines

One decision that organizations must make is whether or not participation in the program should be voluntary. That is, it should be determined if individuals will have a choice as to whether or not they are included and must participate in the program. It is commonly thought that participation in formal mentoring programs should be voluntary. In one review of program practices, it was found that only one out of 56 programs made mentor participation mandatory and only three out of 50 programs made protégé participation mandatory.[1] The argument supporting this recommendation is that people who participate voluntarily will be more committed to making the program, as well as the mentoring experience, more successful than those who are coerced into participation. Those who are required to participate may harbor feelings of resentment at having their time and energy infringed upon, thus reducing their efforts and dedication. This may be especially true for mentors who possibly will view participating in the program as a chore while protégés view it as more of a benefit. Support for advocating voluntary participation also comes from the training and development literature, which shows that giving employees a choice with regard to participation in training activities has a positive effect on outcomes such as motivation to learn.[2]

Despite this generally accepted wisdom, the research evidence with regard to mentoring and voluntary participation is equivocal. Two studies have found no differences in protégé perceptions of overall program effectiveness between protégés whose participation in the program was voluntary versus protégés whose participation in the program was not voluntary.[3] A third study indicated no relationship between protégé reports of mentoring provided (i.e., career and psychosocial mentoring) and whether or not participation was voluntary.[4] However, in an investigation that focused on mentors, mentors who perceived their participation was more voluntary also reported that the mentoring experience was more rewarding than did mentors who perceived their participation was not voluntary.[5] In another study, it was found that protégés reported greater program effectiveness when they thought that their mentors in the program were volunteers than when they thought their mentors were not volunteers.[6] In sum, there is no research to suggest that protégés are affected by the voluntary/involuntary nature of the program. On the other hand, there may be positive effects for mentors' voluntary participation and negative effects on protégés if mentors are not voluntary program participants.

Practical considerations and business issues should be taken into account when determining whether participation should be voluntary or not. For example, a formal mentoring program designed to introduce high potential employees to other senior leaders and expose them to strategic-level work may include only those protégés who *want* to advance in their careers. On the other hand, a mentoring program designed to orient and socialize newly hired MBA graduates may make protégé participation in the mentoring program a condition of employment. A similar approach was utilized by one of the companies profiled in this book – all new hires were assigned a mentor and had to participate; mentors, on the other hand were given a choice as whether or not to participate.

In summary, research focusing directly on mentoring is not clear on whether participation should be mandatory, though research from other areas (e.g., training and development) indicates voluntary participation should be beneficial. If an organization makes mentoring program participation mandatory, we recommend that: (1) it provides the reasons for mandatory participation; (2) it outlines the benefits of participation (to build commitment); and (3) it ensures training is in place to build the proper knowledge, skills, and abilities needed to take advantage of mentoring relationships.

 ## Case Study:
Lessons Learned

One company noted that its original mentoring program mandated that *all* executives within its planning group serve as mentors, as a way of showing strong support and commitment. However, a key learning point was that not all of the executives had the time, skills, or ability to be an effective mentor. Thus, the program evolved to encourage, rather than mandate, executives to be mentors and has adapted its focus from one of "every executive should have a protégé" to one of "every protégé should have a mentor."

Protégé Selection

As mentioned earlier, protégé selection will be driven directly by program goals and objectives. Two issues need to be considered: (1) which overall group or group(s) of employees should be targeted?; and (2) within a particular group, which specific employees should participate? Criteria for protégé selection are often based on membership in a target group for which the program was designed. For example, within programs that are focused on developing future leaders and managers, high potential employees and those who are ready for a promotion may be identified as potential protégés. Other programs may include all employees with less than two years' experience while still another may be restricted to specific populations such as women or minorities. In one review it was reported that the top four groups that organizations targeted mentoring programs for were new hires, anyone in the organization, high-potential employees, and those in professional and managerial ranks. However, some used a subset of one or more groups (e.g., newly hired women and minorities) or multiple groups.[7] It should be noted that if the program is limited to certain groups, care should be taken to try and avoid creating resentment among those who are excluded. Some companies, for example, try not to advertise or publicize their programs for fear of appearing biased or exclusionary. Making sure that employees are aware of the various career development opportunities that exist within the organization that are open and available to all employees may also help mitigate concerns regarding targeted programs.

After determining which group or groups are to receive mentoring, a process must be put into place for selecting individuals from within these groups for participation in the program. As noted earlier, most organizations allow people to volunteer to become protégés. In many programs, meeting basic entry requirements is enough for an employee to become a protégé. For example, as long as a person is a newly hired employee, he or she can self-select to become a protégé in a program targeted to this population. However, in other cases it may be necessary for companies to use additional criteria. This may be due to the particular focus of the program. For example, if a program's purpose is to groom high potential employees for succession planning purposes, there may be a nomination process that could include input from senior management, immediate supervisors, and program administrators. Using additional criteria for protégé selection may also be necessary if an organization is trying to limit the number of protégés entering the program due to a small pool of available mentors.

When screening criteria are necessary, there are a number of different factors that might be considered. A review of 21 different programs indicated that just over 60% screen employees on such factors as potential for advancement, desire to participate, tenure, and interests and goals.[8] Protégé characteristics may be classified into those that are skill-based, motivation-based, and personality-based. In the box below we provide examples of potential protégé characteristics within each of these categories that may be considered by organizations as screening criteria. We emphasize the fact that these should only be considered as *potential* characteristics as the research in this area is limited.

Sample Protégé Screening Criteria

Skill-based

- Listening and communication skills
- Interpersonal skills

Motivation-based

- Willingness to learn
- Need for achievement
- Learning goal orientation
- Job involvement
- Initiative
- Engages in career planning activities
- Self-efficacy for development

Personality-based

- Proactive personality
- Extraversion
- Openness to experience

Some research has examined how personal characteristics might relate to protégé mentoring experience. One investigation of an assigned mentoring program designed for educators found that protégés who were more highly involved in career planning and had greater job involvement were more likely to report receiving more psychosocial mentoring from their mentors than were protégés with lower levels of career planning and job involvement, but no relationship was found with perceptions of the overall quality of the relationship.[9] In another study of formal mentoring relationships, neither protégé proactive personality nor openness to experience related to mentoring outcomes.[10] Other studies based on informal or nonspecific mentoring relationships have found that characteristics such as learning goal orientation, self-esteem, extraversion, and openness to experience positively relate to reports of mentoring received.[11] These are characteristics that might predispose and/or prepare individuals to be more receptive or ready for mentoring. For example, a protégé with a strong learning goal orientation may evoke greater mentoring from his or her mentor because he or she is more goal-directed in his or her interactions with the mentor. However, we have no research evidence to date to suggest that certain qualities make individuals "better or worse" suited for formal mentoring programs.

On the other hand, meta-analytic research in the training and development field has demonstrated that motivation to learn is positively associated with trainee skill and knowledge acquisition, reactions to training, self-efficacy, and transfer of knowledge.[12] This study also found that having an internal locus of control, high achievement motivation, and low anxiety positively related to motivation to learn. Given the importance of motivation to learn for an individual to benefit from the experience as a protégé, these are factors that companies could review in determining who will be protégés in formal mentoring programs.

Other research has asked mentors what makes for an attractive protégé. These characteristics may also be worth considering when evaluating individuals for their suitability as a protégé. As we discuss in the next section, screening protégés for factors that mentors consider attractive may positively impact mentor recruitment. A summary of existing research on this issue is provided in the box below.

Good to Know:

Protégé Characteristics Mentors Find Attractive[13]

- Openness and willingness to learn
- Strong work ethic
- High ability and potential
- Interpersonally skilled

- Trustworthy
- Achievement oriented
- Willingness to accept and act upon constructive feedback

Finally, when deciding on what characteristics to screen for in selecting protégés, it is important to remember that mentoring is a relational learning process. Thus, personal characteristics that predispose an individual to succeed at relationship building, such as interpersonal skills, seem likely to enhance the likelihood that someone will benefit from a mentoring experience. Good interpersonal skills include being sensitive to the feelings of others, the accurate interpretation of emotions, and the ability to effectively resolve conflict.

Once criteria are determined, a process should be implemented for making selection decisions. For example, potential protégés could complete an application. Interviews and letters of recommendation may also be used to select protégés. Or, a cross-functional committee could be used that reviews employees' development plans and their mentoring applications, along with human resources and organizational planning information, to determine who is selected as a protégé. Appendix D provides a sample protégé screening tool that can be adapted for completion by either the potential protégé or by an evaluation committee/supervisor. Psychometrically validated self-report measures of many of the traits and characteristics listed earlier are readily available within the industrial/organizational psychology literature.[14]

Mentor Recruitment

Recruitment of mentors is often a challenge. Potential mentors are hard to find, and among those who are willing, not all will be effective in the mentoring role. The kind of successful individuals who often make the most ideal mentors are also those likely to be extremely busy with many competing demands on their time. Indeed, potential mentors report that one of the biggest obstacles to becoming a mentor to others is the drain on their time.[15]

The early stages and initial formation of the program may be the most difficult time to recruit mentors. Often little is known about mentoring, and the new program is unproven and unknown. Once the mentoring program has been in place, former mentors can be good recruiters by sharing their positive experiences as mentors in the program. Additionally, research consistently shows that the best predictor of who is willing to be a mentor is someone with previous mentoring experience as either a mentor or as a protégé.[16] Individuals who have been protégés often want to give back because they have experienced the power of mentoring.

When developing a mentor recruitment strategy it is important to consider why individuals would want to be a mentor to others. Research suggests there are three primary reasons why mentors mentor: (1) the desire to benefit the organization and its members; (2) intrinsic satisfaction; and (3) the desire to enhance one's own standing within the organization.[17] For example, listed in the box below are the results of one study that assessed reasons for mentoring. This information can be communicated to potential mentors as a

---

Good to Know:
Reasons to Become a Mentor[19]

- You will be doing something good for others.
- You will have the opportunity to pass along the knowledge and information that you have accumulated.
- You will help build the organization.
- You will learn new information and develop your own skills.

- You will create positive energy and satisfaction for yourself through the experience of helping someone else grow and develop in the organization.
- You may be recognized by your peers and higher level individuals within the organization.
- You may improve your own job performance.

way to get individuals to think about why they may want to become part of the mentoring program. Another important benefit to mentoring others is that it has been associated with higher supervisory ratings of performance.[18] Specifically, in a global study of managers conducted by the Center for Creative Leadership, managers who provided greater career-related mentoring were rated by their supervisors as better performers than were managers who provided less career-related mentoring. Communicating to potential mentors the benefits of mentoring others, for themselves, for the organization, and for the protégé, may expand the pool of willing mentors.

As mentioned in Chapter 2, there is no evidence that programs geared toward one type of objective are perceived as more effective than those geared toward another type of objective.[20] We are not aware of any studies that compare the success of general programs to those that target specific groups, such as fast-trackers, newcomers, or individuals in need of remediation. Thus, at this point we cannot conclude that programs with a targeted population help participants better than do broad-based programs. However, the purpose of the program may impact the type of mentors that are drawn to it. As noted earlier, research has shown that, in general, mentors are more drawn to protégés with high potential and ability rather than those in need of help. Thus, it may be that programs with a more remedial focus may have a more difficult time attracting mentors than do programs targeting fast-trackers or other high potential employees.[21] It may be worth considering the characteristics that mentors have reported most desirable in protégés that were noted in the previous section. The quality of the protégés in the program may impact the desire of individuals to accept the role of mentor. Keep in mind that individuals may be more willing to be a mentor when the pool of protégés are perceived as high quality and, most importantly, as "coachable." Mentors want to work with individuals who they believe have the ability to benefit from the experience and who are open and receptive to learning.

Some thought and planning should also be given to sustaining the commitment of mentors over time. Mentors are more likely to stay part of the program when they have self-efficacy and when they believe that they are well prepared for their role as a mentor. Mentor self-efficacy and preparation can be heightened with training (see

Chapter 5). Support groups for mentors also serve as a means to reinforce the role identity of mentors, which has been shown as a key way to sustain volunteerism in other contexts.[22] Finally, the evaluation process (see Chapter 7) should be used not only to assess protégé satisfaction with the program, but mentor satisfaction as well. Retention of mentors will be greater when their own needs are also being met within the program. Finally, as illustrated in the case study below, providing recognition and rewards can be an effective tool for maintaining a steady pool of willing mentors.

Case Study:
Recognizing Mentors

As a way to help recognize and reward the efforts of mentors, KPMG has introduced a national mentoring award. All employees were asked to nominate mentors they believed had helped in a truly meaningful way. For 2007, the firm received over 800 nominations. In January (National Mentoring Month) 14 award winners were announced. There was considerable acknowledgment and visibility given to the winners, including dinner with the operations committee. In addition, on January 25 (National Mentoring Day), the company sent out an electronic thank you letter to all 800 nominees. On the nomination forms there was a line asking for 2-3 sentences on "what would you say to thank your mentor?". The lines provided by the nominees were included in the electronic thank you.

Mentor Selection

Mentors form the backbone of formal mentoring programs. Indeed, any formal mentoring program is only as good as the mentors that participate in it. Research has indicated that mentor characteristics are the most influential factor affecting the quality of the mentoring experience.[23] Thus, the selection of mentors is an issue that should receive careful attention.

Most organizations use experienced professionals, managers, and executives. Other organizations allow anyone to be a mentor or restrict mentor participation to certain groups depending upon the objectives of the program (e.g., minorities; functional managers). In a review of industry practices, it was found that over two-thirds of responding companies screen their potential mentors for several criteria, including technical knowledge, communication ability, organizational level and tenure, past performance, commitment to the mentoring process, credibility, and ability to be an effective role model.[24] Although it may be tempting to permit anyone who volunteers to mentor others to do so, we advocate that mentors be screened for suitability.

The first factor to consider when selecting mentors is the needs of the protégés to be targeted in the program. For example, different mentor criteria may be called upon for programs with the purpose of new employee socialization (e.g., interpersonal skills, strong network) versus programs with the purpose of succession planning (e.g., coaching skills, development planning ability). Beyond that, additional factors to consider when identifying and selecting mentors include their experience and expertise, their knowledge, skills, abilities and other characteristics (KSAOs) such as interest and motivation.

Several research studies have identified characteristics thought to be important to effective mentoring based on subject matter expert assessments (e.g., experienced mentors; program administrators).[25] The common characteristics identified are shown in the box below.

Good to Know:
Mentor Knowledge, Skills, and Abilities

- Empathy
- Ability to role model behaviors the organization wants emulated
- Confidence
- Listening and communication skills
- Technical knowledge
- Credibility
- Commitment

- Enjoy helping others
- Patience
- Ability to read and understand others
- Credible and trustworthy
- Interpersonal skills/ability to work well with others
- Ability to teach, provide direction and guidance
- Willing to share knowledge

Some research has provided greater substantiation for specific characteristics by linking them with mentoring outcomes. One characteristic often mentioned by experts and that is supported by the research literature is empathy.[26] An empathetic mentor demonstrates acceptance of the protégé and enjoys helping others. Also, in a study of formal mentoring, mentor proactive personality was related to the amount of mentoring reported by both mentors and protégés.[27] Individuals with a proactive personality look for better ways to do things, actively champion ideas, and demonstrate persistence when faced with opposition from others.

Lessons Learned

- Make sure the protégés who participate in the program are willing to shoulder much of the responsibility for making the relationship work.
- Make sure the mentors are willing and have the time needed to devote to the relationship.
- Do not force people to mentor who do not have the time, motivation, or ability.

Finally, it is absolutely critical that mentors have a high level of interest and motivation in the formal mentoring program. Logically, motivated mentors will make more of an effort to honor scheduled appointments, provide protégés with guidance, and make the relationship successful. Organizations should ensure that the mentor has enough time to commit to the relationship and that they are willing to participate for the "right" reasons (e.g., desire to help others develop), rather than because of pressure from top management. Recent research has shown that mentor commitment, as perceived by protégés, relates to protégé reports of satisfaction with the mentoring program and to satisfaction with the mentoring relationship.[28] Practically speaking, this suggests that, in most circumstances, mentors be allowed to voluntary participate in a mentoring program, even when protégé participation may be mandatory. Appendix C presents a sample "Mentor Readiness Assessment Form" that companies can use to help their potential mentors assess whether they have the time, energy, and skills to be effective mentors. This can be tailored to reflect various programs' mentoring goals.

Action Plan:
Participant Recruitment and Selection

- Narrow down the pool of potential protégés depending on the goal of the program and the target number of protégés desired, given resources.
- Within this pool, determine if protégé selection will be voluntary or mandatory.
- Determine protégé screening criteria and how to measure those criteria.
- Screen protégés and select final pool.
- Determine the qualities needed in mentors based on the goal of the program.
- Determine number of mentors needed based on the number of protégés.
- Recruit potential mentors.
- Determine mentor screening criteria and how to measure those criteria.
- Screen potential mentors.
- At this stage, consider retaining more than the number of mentors you will ultimately need, to provide more flexibility at the matching stage.

Chapter 4

Matching Mentors and Protégés

One defining feature that distinguishes formal mentoring from informal mentoring is that in formal mentoring programs, mentors and protégés are usually matched with some involvement from the organization. However, the practice of matching protégés and mentors has been a common criticism of formal mentoring programs, in that no one can "force" the natural attraction and desire to work together that is essential for mentorships to flourish and be successful. Forced pairing, if not done well, can contribute to resentment, hurt feelings, and suspicion. Indeed, in one study of formal mentoring, the most common problem noted by both mentors and protégés was mentor–protégé mismatch.[1]

Why is the match so important? The quality of the bond formed between the mentor and the protégé will have a substantial impact on any positive outcomes that are to result from the mentoring engagement. Mentoring is first and foremost a relationship. Stronger alliances, typified by high commitment, open communication, and concern for the welfare of the other partner, contribute to enhanced outcomes. The matching process may be the single most important factor contributing to a successful mentoring relationship, but one in which we have the least research evidence to provide guidance.

It is our contention that there is no single best way to match mentors and protégés that will work equally well for all program purposes and for all organizations. In that vein, this chapter follows a somewhat different format from the other chapters. We begin the chapter with an in-depth analysis of the experiences involving matching mentors and protégés reported by organizations operating successful mentoring programs garnered through our case study interviews. Our intent is to help readers discover the many considerations and approaches other organizations have taken. After summarizing the findings from our interviews, we return to the usual format of the other chapters and provide step-by-step coverage of the key issues with inclusion of supporting research findings. Specifically, we discuss: (1) input into matching; (2) matching characteristics; and (3) specific suggestions intended to help tie all of the information together. Throughout the chapter we outline various factors to consider, illustrate different approaches taken by companies, and provide some advantages and disadvantages to each of the approaches considered.

Overview of Approaches to the Match Process

Research concerning actual practices within industry indicates that a variety of methods are used to match mentors and protégés. Organizations also vary in their philosophy with regard to issues such as matching mentors and protégés from different departments, geographic locations, and functional areas. Consistent with past research and writing, our case study interviews with companies that have formal programs revealed no one "best" process or method for matching mentors with protégés. In most cases the matching method used by a company flowed generally from the goals of the program and the culture of the organization. Still, we were able to identify several dimensions that characterize the processes used by companies to match.

Formality of Matching Process

Even though each company has formalized their overall mentoring program as well as particular features of the program (e.g., structuring the relationship), companies differed on the degree of formality they used to match protégés with mentors. Quest, for example, uses a structured approach whereby protégés and mentors are screened against multiple criteria, and a computer algorithm is used to identify the two best mentor matches for a protégé. From there the protégé interviews both potential mentors (after receiving interview training on which types of questions to ask) and selects the mentor thought to be the best fit. At a global energy company, after completing a formal process to identify and screen both potential mentors and protégés, a multiple step process is used for matching. First the program administrators will review the available information, and consider recommendations and input from multiple stakeholders (e.g., Human Resources personnel, protégé's boss), to make final matching recommendations. These recommendations are then presented to and discussed with the executive committee overseeing the program, who then makes the final matching decisions.

At a pharmaceutical company, executive committee members each nominate two or three high potential protégés and identify their strengths and developmental needs. In collaboration with senior HR leaders, potential protégés are then reviewed and ranked to determine who has the highest priority for mentoring. Each executive committee member is then matched with a protégé for a one-year one-on-one mentoring relationship. A similar process is used in Citi's program, where HR Heads representing executive-level mentors generate and present a list of up to four potential protégés. A round-table discussion ensues whereby each HR Head discusses the protégé's background, strengths, development needs, and career aspirations, using development plans and management profiles as well as that of the executive committee member. Based on this discussion and the consideration of a broad range of factors, matches are decided.

On the other hand, to fit its culture, Weyerhauser does not utilize a highly formal matching process. Rather, it allows protégés to either choose their own mentor, or to work with a manager or employee support network to locate a mentor. Human Resources, for example, can provide assessments and guidance to help protégés make an effective decision regarding who will be their mentor. Similarly, given the size and scope of KPMG's mentoring program (available to all employees), protégés are encouraged to identify and procure their own mentors, with assistance from Human Resources or management as needed.

Characteristics Used to Match

Companies varied in the types of personal characteristics used when matching protégés and mentors, the total number of personal characteristics used, as well as which characteristics were emphasized more than others. Quest's computer algorithm approach, for example, weighs such factors as the protégé's competency evaluation, interests, geographical information, and other logistical issues, in determining an effective mentor–protégé match. When possible, diversity within the match is preferred. The mentors have a comparable profile in the system and the development needs and career goals of the protégé are pre-matched with the mentor's experience and expertise. Citi's program bases its formal matching decisions upon a broad range of factors, including the protégé's developmental needs and career aspirations, time zone differences between the mentor and the protégé, functional responsibilities of the mentor and the protégé, and personal characteristics. Likewise, a global energy company balances the protégé's development needs, personality compatibility, reporting relationships, and personal interests when matching mentors and protégés.

On the other hand, the matching process described by some companies tends to focus on one or two factors. For example, Starwood Hotels' property managers base their matching decisions primarily on the mentor's ability to address the protégé's competencies that need development, although other factors such as the protégé's functional responsibilities and personality fit are sometimes considered. Advocate Health Center's physician on-boarding program focuses primarily on pairing mentors and protégés within the same hospital, but at times demographics and physician specialty can factor into the decision. When geographical and travel issues are a concern, it was important to have a close match in location in order to facilitate more personal contact time between the mentor and protégé. In KPMG, when Human Resources or management becomes involved in locating a suitable mentor, the match generally rests on the protégé's needs and what he or she wants out of the relationship. At a pharmaceutical company, matching decisions rest primarily on pairing employees from different functions and on which mentor can best address the protégé's strengths and developmental needs.

Participant Input

Companies differed regarding the degree of latitude they provide mentors and protégés to identify potential partners and determine with whom they will be paired. In some companies, for example, the protégé is given significant latitude to choose who will be his or her mentor. As described earlier, at Quest the protégé interviews two potential mentors and selects the best fit for him or her. Similarly, Weyerhauser's program allows its protégés to locate and choose their mentors, with or without assistance from others. Given the size of KPMG's mentoring program, and the fact that mentoring is so readily accepted within its culture, in most instances protégés will seek out their own mentors, although they can use Human Resources or management assistance if needed. At KPMG, managers are also provided training on how to say "no" when requested to be a mentor if they are overloaded with work or have too many other protégés.

Other organizations provide a balance between incorporating participants' input vs. having an external party make the matching decision. In one major aerospace corporation's Human Resources mentoring program, for example, the protégé can choose up to three names of potential mentors who are internal to Human Resources, if possible. The potential mentors are then contacted to gauge their interest. Using this information, a Human Resources matching committee will review information about the protégé's background, education, work experience, and desired benefits from the mentoring relationship, review the list of mentors, and make the most effective match.

At a pharmaceutical company, the executive committee will nominate a list of high potential protégés, identify their key strengths and developmental needs, and decide who from the committee will mentor each protégé. The name of the mentor and the developmental issues to be addressed during the relationship are then conveyed to the protégé. Citi uses a similar approach in one of its divisions. Specifically, each HR Head, representing executive-level mentors nominates up to four potential protégés and, through discussion and review of certain criteria, matching decisions are made. Thus, in these programs it is the mentors who determine the matching decision and what issues will be addressed.

Some companies, on the other hand, place the majority of match decision-making responsibility in an external party's hands. For example, a global energy company does not typically seek the protégé's input, reasoning that the protégé may not have the knowledge and insight of the company needed in order to determine who best can help him or her with their developmental challenges. However, protégés do provide quarterly feedback on how the relationship is progressing and can request a different mentor if the relationship is not meeting their needs. Similarly, at Miller Brewing Company, mentors and protégés typically do not have input into who will be their partner in order that the program administrators can base their decision solely on the protégés' needs and goals. Within Advocate Health Center's physician medical group, most matching decision-making responsibility falls on the shoulders of each location's Medical Director with some input from the participants.

Standardization of Decision-Making

The degree that companies' matching recommendations were based on a standardized decision-making process appeared to differ. Again, in many instances the process used seemed to flow from the goals of the program, as well as how structured the matching process was in general. Simply having a standardized method for matching does not ensure success, as companies with less stringent guidelines also reported success.

The use of computer programs and algorithms is a method that some companies, Quest, for example, use to increase the level of objectivity and analysis in their matching recommendations. Similarly, another company measures and evaluates several characteristics of its potential mentors and protégés (e.g., training and experience; validated personality assessments; potential for success). This information is then entered into a computerized database, which has a search function allowing the user to obtain a short list of possible matches based on the information described above. Starwood Hotels also provides its property managers and participants with the opportunity to use an electronic system to review the participants' competencies and other information in order to make effective matches.

At Miller Brewing Company, a standardized process is used to screen potential protégés, weighing, for example, factors such as potential to advance, diversity issues, interest in development, and ability to participate. From there, protégés report the five issues, out of a list of 20, that they want to work on, and the protégé is then paired with the executive mentor who is most capable of helping the protégé with his or her developmental challenges.

Other companies appeared to take a less structured approach to weighing factors and evidence. At Advocate Health Center, for example, which has multiple medical practice locations with multiple Medical Directors, the matching decision will often become a judgment call from the Director weighing multiple factors and the needs of the situation and facility, in no pre-set manner. At companies that give most of the matching recommendation responsibility to the mentor and/or protégé (e.g., KPMG), it is left up to the individuals to determine which factors they want to consider as well as how that information is weighted.

In sum, there are a variety of approaches that can be used to match mentors and protégés. In the following sections, we review key considerations and provide guidance based on the empirical research literature.

Input into Matching

In terms of program design, a key question is 'who will determine the match?' There is some presumption that informal or naturally occurring mentoring relationships work best because the mentor and the protégé choose each other. That is, there is some mutual attraction that brings the two together. To make an effort to capitalize on the potential of chemistry between the participants, some programs implement an element of choice into the formal matching process.

Third party matching systems are not an unusual concept within the relationship domain. For example, in some cultures the responsibility for mate selection is in the hands of outside parties, ranging from family, elders, and professional matchmakers.[2] Various services exist solely to create interpersonal matches, from the Shadkhan, or Jewish matchmaker, to marriage bureaus popular in England, to video and/or computer dating services. The role and authority of the individual in such cases can vary from none to highly involved with veto power.[3] For example, some online matching services leave it completely up to participants to contact each other while other services such as *eHarmony* create a personality profile matching system to narrow down choices for each client, thereby taking a more active role in determining the user's choice. Similarly, as illustrated in the previous section, organizations vary regarding the degree that they manage the pairing process versus how much control is given to participants. One study of industry practices indicated that 75% of companies use a structured matching procedure.[4]

Many reasons have been suggested as to why giving program participants input into the match process should be an important program feature. As noted previously, it has been suggested that allowing mentors and protégés some discretion in selecting their partner likens the formal match more closely to an informal match that would develop naturally. Such a process may foster employee ownership and thus more commitment to the mentoring program. The research evidence on this issue is mixed, but generally favors giving participants input. In one study, there was no evidence to support the notion that protégés in formal programs in which participant match input occurred were more satisfied than those in programs in which no input occurred.[5] Likewise, in a study focusing on mentors, no mentoring benefits were associated with input into the match.[6] On the other hand, in another study, both mentors' and protégés' reports of greater input into the matching process related to their reports of program effectiveness. Input into the match was also associated with enhanced mentor commitment and program understanding. Having some say regarding who one's mentoring partner is facilitates perceptions that the mentor is psychologically engaged in the relationship.[7] Another study of formal mentoring in public accounting firms reported that protégés who had at least some input into the match process were significantly more satisfied with the relationship than were those who had no say.[8]

From these studies we might conclude that "some say" in the match process is helpful. However, *how much* say is necessary is uncertain. For example, we do not know if it is enough to allow mentoring participants to choose from a few criteria to narrow down the pool from which one's partner will be drawn, or if it is advisable for the participants to meet in advance and get to know one another. Furthermore, when mentors and/or protégés do get to choose the partner, we do not know the typical characteristics on which they are likely to base their choice and if those used are those that are the most important to the company. Finally, we do not know if there are benefits to protégé input versus mentor input or if a balance between the two is needed. Some qualitative research data based on mentors interviewed from formal programs indicates that mentors believe that the weight of the decision should be given to the protégé and that their preferences and needs should be given high priority.[9]

Research from the domain of participative decision-making (PDM) also supports the point of view that giving participants input into the match process may be beneficial. In general, PDM refers to involving employees in making decisions on issues that are normally the responsibility of management. Allowing participants a choice in their mentoring partner can be considered a form of PDM. Many reviews of years of research and meta-analyses on PDM suggest that there may be a significant, but small relationship between PDM and organizational outcomes such as job performance and job satisfaction.[10]

There are several factors to consider when determining the potential effectiveness of participation. If participation is standard with regard to other aspects of organizational life, then more active participation as part of the formal mentoring program may also be expected by participants.[11] Another factor to consider is national culture. Specifically, companies that intend to develop mentoring programs across multinational locations should be aware that not all cultures appear to be accepting of participation in decision-making, and that the form that PDM takes may vary widely across cultures.[12] Cultural dimensions such as collectivism and power distance should be considered. For example, in collectivist cultures, individuals may wish to make decisions regarding matching in a group format that takes into account the needs of all protégés simultaneously. In high power distance cultures, in which there is a sharp distinction between those who are in positions of authority and those who are not, it may be generally less accepted to give participants input into decisions.

It should also be noted that another possible method for pairing mentors and protégés is through random assignment. Random assignment has been likened to the blind date and associated with a number of pitfalls.[13] It is rarely successful. Systematic matching can do more to increase success levels. Not surprisingly, few companies actually do random assignments when matching. We too recommend against this method of mentor–protégé matching.

In sum, the best level of participation in the matching process is not yet clear. The limited empirical literature shows that some input into the match has yielded benefits. We also know that the effects of participative decision-making are modest. A company should consider its climate and culture to help determine when and for whom participation in the match will make an ultimate difference in satisfaction with a program.

Matching Characteristics

Organizations face a huge challenge in determining what characteristics they want to consider when determining how to match mentors and protégés. Matching is important in that satisfaction with the match has been associated more favorable evaluations of the overall program and to increased relationship quality for both mentors and protégés.[14]

However, the research on effective matching processes is sparse with little data to guide organizations. Even the literature on formal mentoring programs for youth, which is far more advanced in terms of rigorous evaluation of best practices than is the workplace mentoring literature, is equivocal regarding the best basis for matching mentors and protégés.[15]

Some lessons for workplace mentoring programs can be learned with regard to matching from the well-established youth mentoring program, Big Brothers/Big Sisters (BBBS). Although there are substantial differences in goals and objectives between BBBS and workplace mentoring programs, the objective of developing a less experienced and/or disadvantaged individual is one that is shared. The approach taken by BBBS conforms to the "responsivity principle." This principle suggests that protégés should be matched to mentors who possess personal traits that may influence protégés' response to the mentors. In organizations another way to think about this is that mentors and protégés should be paired in a way that helps facilitate the development of a bond between the mentoring partners while also achieving the purpose and objectives of the program. This should be an overarching factor considered throughout the matching process.

What Participants Want in Terms of Matching

In an evaluation study of a formal mentoring program for junior university faculty, protégés were asked the extent that they thought each of six factors should be taken into account when matching mentors and protégés.[16] The six factors were: research interests, work styles, nonwork interests, values, personality, and demographics/ background. Results indicated the following order in terms of preferences: research interests, work styles, values, demographics/ background, personalities, and nonwork interests. In this study, the following results were also reported by protégés:

- Matches based on work styles were related to more help from the mentor in meeting the protégé's goals.
- Matches based on nonwork interests or on values were related to more favorable evaluations of the program, higher relationship quality, and more help from the mentor in meeting the protégé's goals.
- Matches based on personality were related to more favorable evaluations of the program and higher relationship quality.
- Matches based upon demographics or background characteristics were not related to the program and relationship outcomes.

Data from another study that investigated a mentoring program for university faculty showed somewhat similar results. For protégés, the factors considered most important were personality, ability to pick mentor, mentor rank, research interests, and field of study. Least important were gender, marital status, and parental status. Most important to mentors were field, personality, rank, and ability to pick. Least important were research interests, parental status, marital status, and gender.[17] In sum, mentors and protégés in these faculty settings expressed more interest in being matched based on personality, work styles, and content areas of importance than based on demographic factors.

Similarity

A great deal has been written regarding the role of similarity in mentoring relationships. Perceived mentor–protégé similarity has been consistently associated with greater mentoring provided and stronger relationship quality.[18] Perceived mismatches in terms of values, personality, and work styles have been identified as barriers to relationship effectiveness by both protégés and mentors.[19] The importance of similarity in dating relationships has been a mainstay in social psychology. Years of research support the notion that "birds of a feather flock together," over the "opposites attract" argument.[20]

Similarity in terms of mentoring relationships is a broad concept. It could be based on more surface-level, demographic characteristics, but it could also be based on a host of other shared qualities that range from common leisure interests to similar work styles to compatible personality traits. Similarity can be assessed subjectively or objectively. Subjective assessments are those that simply ask the participants the extent that they believe that they are similar to their mentoring partners. Objective assessments involve the actual comparison of mentors and protégés on the variable of interest. For example, both mentors and protégés may complete a personality assessment and those who both score as extraverted may be considered as similar to each other from an objective perspective. Interestingly, perceived similarity is often unrelated to objective similarity. Moreover, perceptions of being similar are often more important than are objective indicators of similarity in terms of predicting relationship quality.[21] One practical implication of these findings is that if perceived similarities between mentoring partners can be elicited, any potential relational problems stemming from true differences may be minimized.

On the other hand, there may be value in matching individuals who are dissimilar on some characteristics. One theoretical perspective is that matching mentors and protégés on the basis of similarity will enhance rapport within the relationship while matching on the basis of dissimilarity will support learning within the relationship.[22] For example, organizations often intentionally match formal mentors and protégés from different departments or business units in an effort to enhance learning. Similarly, a company may intentionally match an extraverted mentor with an introverted protégé, if one of the purposes of the relationship is to help the protégé become more outgoing. Matching an introvert with an introvert may prove difficult in terms of facilitating relational bonding. Thus, the pressing question that emerges is, "On what characteristics should mentors and protégés be similar and on what characteristics should they be dissimilar to maximize the success of formal mentoring programs?"

Part of the answer to this question may lie in knowing what the goals are for the relationship. In other words, there may be situations where similarity (or dissimilarity) is more or less important. For instance, if the protégé hopes the mentor will be able to be a sounding board and provide friendship, then similarity with regard to personality may be particularly important to foster identification and liking. In contrast, if the protégé enters the program to gain a better understanding of the organization and learn new skills to prepare him or her for upward mobility, then dissimilarity with the mentor, particularly in terms of job type, background, and educational specialty may become key to facilitating that goal.

It is also probably safe to assert that the purpose of the program should be taken into account when deciding on the matching approach to use. For example, if a program is designed to enhance the understanding of different areas of the business, matching individuals from different functional areas would likely help accomplish such goals. However, if the purpose of a program is to develop the leadership skills of junior employees within a specific function, such as Supply Chain Management, then pairing those employees with senior leaders from within Supply Chain Management (*similarity of function*), but who have different and greater leadership skill sets (*dissimilarity of skills*), may prove beneficial. Below are some examples:

- Someone has been working in the commercial business in the US, and needs more global exposure. Pairing this individual with an internationally-based mentor within the commercial business might be one option to achieve this goal.
- Someone has worked in the legal function but needs a broader view of the commercial business and sales arena. Matching the participant with someone from the Sales and Marketing area might prove beneficial.
- Someone is effective at execution and getting results from direct reports, but needs to understand how to influence and impact when not in a position of direct supervisory control. Pairing this person with someone who leads within a matrix management structure (e.g., a Project Manager) could help this person develop such skills.

A study of common industry practices found a fairly close split between programs that matched protégés and mentors based on criteria similarity and those that matched based on dissimilarity. For example, depending on the program's objectives, some companies choose to have mentors and protégés from the same functional area, whereas other companies match protégés and mentors from different functions.[23]

Demographic Characteristics

The matching of mentors and protégés based on demographic characteristics such as race and gender has been the topic of research, with results indicating that these factors are not consistently associated with relationship outcomes. Despite these equivocal findings, we recommend that some special attention to cross-race and cross-gender matches be given. For example, participants in cross-race relationships should have a good appreciation for other racial cultural backgrounds and have the interpersonal skills to demonstrate sensitivity. Racial similarity may not be so important as is similarity regarding attitudes regarding race and racial issues. Similarity in terms of attitudes can help facilitate the interpersonal bonding process.[24] Cross-gender mentoring pairs can face unique challenges such as jealousy from spouses and sexual innuendo from others. Additionally, cross-gender pairs may feel less comfortable engaging in after-work social activities, resulting in a restriction of the more psychosocial forms of mentoring behaviors. Some research suggests that increasing interpersonal comfort within cross-gender pairs is the key to mitigating this potential problem.[25] Methods to increase interpersonal comfort while minimizing concerns regarding innuendo within cross-gender relationships can be addressed during training (see Chapter 5). Some strategies include engaging in mutual sharing of information that can reveal dimensions of similarity and common ground, setting boundaries for conversation, and getting to know each other's family.[26]

Rank

One factor often considered with respect to matching mentors and protégés is the difference in hierarchical level. Some recommend having a mentor of significantly higher rank than the protégé in order to augment the likelihood that there will be a sufficient difference in experience and network breadth to be able to provide a protégé with a valuable experience. On the other hand, others have argued that the best mentors are individuals who are only one level higher because they can better relate to the protégé's role requirements, job concerns, responsibilities, obstacles, priorities, and challenges. Empirically, no ideal difference in rank between mentor and protégé has been identified. Data from protégés seem to indicate that mentors closer in rank to the protégé provide more role modeling behaviors than mentors higher in rank relative to the protégé.[27] The authors suggested that protégés may be able to relate to and therefore emulate mentors who are closer to them in rank. In others words, close-in-rank mentors may seem a more realistic model for their immediate aspirations. However, the mentors from this same study reported the opposite findings. Specifically, higher-ranking mentors were more likely to report providing higher levels of role modeling. It may be that mentors may feel better equipped to be a role model when they are more substantially ahead of the protégé in terms of rank. Rank has not been found to relate to protégé perceptions of relationship quality.[28]

Lessons Learned

One company originally intended to have its highest levels of executive leadership mentor high potential, diverse employees. However, it found that these mentors did not always understand the roles and issues faced by these lower-level employees, so that they had difficult relating to and providing feedback to the protégés. The company decided to have mentors that were closer in level to the protégés as a result.

Another company was surprised by some personality conflicts that cropped up within mentoring pairs, and changed their training to encourage mentors and protégés to talk openly about concerns, needs, requirements, and problems upfront rather than let them fester over time. Having mentors and protégés be physically located close to one another was a lesson-learned cited by many companies as well.

Same or Different Department

Another consideration in the match process is whether the mentor and protégé should be from the same or different departments. There are several reasons for recommending that mentors come from different departments than their protégé. One thought is that restricting mentors to the same department as the protégé may limit the potential pool of mentors and thus reduce the likelihood that a good match will occur. Further, a mentor from another department can add fresh perspective and insight. A third factor is that a within-department special and exclusive relationship between a mentor and protégé could create jealousy and departmental conflict. Fourth, restricting mentoring to the same department could increase the likelihood that the mentoring relationship will adversely interact with the protégé's direct supervisory reporting relationship. In some cases the choice may be obvious. For example, programs designed to give protégés exposure to different functional areas may have a clear mandate to make inter-departmental matches. Similarly, a program located mainly within one department (e.g., Human Resources), by default, will match mentors and protégés from the same department, although they can still come from different divisions or functions (e.g., Compensation vs. Recruitment).

Research findings on the topic are again mixed. One study found that having a mentor from a different department was associated with protégé greater organizational commitment, fewer intentions to quit, and stronger satisfaction with the mentor.[29] In another study, protégés reported receiving greater career mentoring from mentors within the *same* department and mentors reported providing more psychosocial mentoring to protégés from the *same* department. These relationships were mediated by interaction frequency suggesting that matching mentors and protégés from the same department has the benefit of enhanced opportunity for interaction, which in turn relates to greater mentoring provided.[30]

Geographic Proximity

An additional variable that can factor into matching is the physical distance between mentor and protégé. Research has indicated that mentors and protégés desire relationships in which they are in close proximity to each other.[31] This appeared to be largely a matter of logistics; close proximity increases the ease of meeting more frequently. The authors of this study also noted that it is possible that mentors in closer proximity to their protégés may be less likely to shirk their mentoring duties if chance "run into each other in the halls" meetings with a protégé could serve as a reminder. Empirical research has not found proximity to be a predictor of mentoring outcomes such as relationship quality, but it has been associated with the frequency with which mentors and protégés report interacting.[32]

Specific Suggestions

Although the current state of research is lacking in some areas, such as which factors are more or less important for ensuring a successful relationship, some specific suggestions in creating the matching process for an organization can be offered. These factors are summarized in the box below and then elaborated on further in the text that follows.

Specific Suggestions for Matching

- Base the matching process on the program's objectives.
- Base the matching process on the company's culture.
- Pair mentors and protégés in close enough physical proximity.
- Pair mentors and protégés not in direct line of supervisory relationship.
- Base the matching decision on multiple factors.
- Ensure rationality and consistency of matching decisions.
- Include some level of "similarity" even for "dissimilar" mentor–protégé relationships.

- *Base the matching process on the program's objectives.* If the purpose of the program is to provide protégés with cross-functional experience and to broaden their business perspective, then it makes logical sense that the company intentionally pair participants from different departments or functions. If the purpose is to provide greater exposure within one's function or department so as to increase career advancement opportunities, then a same-function mentor–protégé relationship may be more advantageous. Similarly, if the program objectives require mentor–protégé matches where the mentors and protégés have had little exposure to one another in the past, then the company may place limits on the input and decision-making responsibility of participants.

- *Base the matching process on the company's culture.* If the company is typically top-down in terms of its rules, decisions, procedures, etc., then it may be more congruent (and acceptable to participants) for the company to restrict participants' input and decision-making responsibility for matching. Conversely, a company that strongly practices participative decision-making should give more decision-making responsibility to participants. Likewise, if the company strongly and purposely promotes diversity in thought, perspective, demographics, etc., then it may encounter more success at intentionally pairing dissimilar mentors and protégés (assuming this would be consistent with the program's goals).

- *Pair mentors and protégés in close enough physical proximity.* A consistent theme in our case study interviews, as well as past research, is that mentors and protégés who are located relatively closely stand greater chances of more frequent interaction, even considering advanced technologies for distance relationships (e.g., web-based conferencing). Personal interaction can increase the likelihood that difficult and/or sensitive issues will be discussed and addressed and can provide the opportunity for open and honest feedback.

- *Pair mentors and protégés not in direct line of supervisory relationship.* For programs where mentors and protégés originate from the same department or function, it is recommended that mentor–protégé dyads not be within the same line of supervision. Not doing so can increase the likelihood that issues discussed and covered in the mentoring relationship could "bleed" over into the protégé's formal job evaluations or administrative decisions.

- *Base the matching decision on multiple factors.* Given the complexity of relationships, even when the purpose of the formal mentoring program seems to call for one or two factors to dominate in a matching decision (e.g., functions in which the mentor and protégé work), we recommend that organizations use multiple factors when matching. As is the case when making selection/hiring decisions, a broad consideration of multiple factors (e.g., goals, interests, skills, abilities, personality, fit, experience) can result in the likelihood that a more effective match will be made. For example, if a protégé from engineering who needs sales experience is matched with a mentor from sales and marketing, that relationship, even though logically based on the most important factor, may not succeed if the two are dissimilar in communication styles or interpersonal values.

- *Ensure rationality and consistency of matching decisions.* Empirical research does not indicate which factors are more or less important in matching. Rather, as we have argued, the factors used should be based on the goals of the program. However, we also believe it is important that whatever process and/or factors a company uses, that they do so rationally and consistently. Specifically, (1) in choosing what factor to use in matching and how that factor is to be used (i.e., match based on similarity and dissimilarity), the company needs to have multiple well-developed business reasons to support its decision; and (2) once implemented, the company should follow the same process for all mentor and protégé matches (as is the case with standardized personnel selection procedures). This will help ensure that the company's matching process is fair, logical, objective, and free from potential bias or conflicts.

- *Include some level of "similarity" even for "dissimilar" mentor–protégé relationships.* As with any type of interpersonal relationship where honest dialogue is to take place, the protégé and mentor need to make a personal "connection" and form some sense of a bond. The importance of quick rapport cannot be overlooked within the often time-limited boundary of a formal mentoring relationship. This connection can be enhanced when the organization matches protégés and mentors on factors that will increase their attraction to one another (cf., "responsivity principle"). These factors can be "dissimilar" in nature (i.e., when the mentor has breadth of experience that the protégé lacks but needs), but organizations should also ensure that "similar" or shared characteristics (e.g., hobbies, interests, background, education, etc.) be used to match protégés and mentors in order that they can form a more common foundation on which to build their relationship.

One method that companies can use to collect relevant matching information is to have mentors and protégés submit a two-page profile. A sample profile form for mentors can be found in Appendix E and a form for protégés can be found in Appendix F. Having obtained this information from the mentor and protégé, the program administrator should ask several probing questions to determine whether a protégé and mentor are an appropriate match. For example,

- Is the mentor senior enough in comparison to the protégé to be a valuable learning resource to the protégé?
- Are the mentor and protégé physically accessible to one another?
- Is the mentor in the right functional area to be useful to the protégé?
- Does the mentor have the skill set needed to meet the developmental needs of the particular protégé?
- Does the mentor have the right connections in order to help the protégé build the network he or she needs?
- Does the mentor have the right combination of knowledge and experiences in order to provide sound instruction, guidance, and wisdom to the protégé?
- Does the protégé possess the characteristics that the mentor described as valuable to him or her?
- Can the barriers to the mentor's participation be overcome?
- Is there enough similarity in backgrounds (e.g., hobbies, interests, education, work experience) to ensure some common ground in the relationship?
- Are the protégé's stated goals consistent with what the mentor can/wants to offer the protégé?
- Can the barriers to the protégé's participation be overcome?
- Does the mentor possess the characteristics desired by the protégé?

Computerized Matching Assistance

The use of computerized algorithms has become an increasingly popular method for matching. Computerized systems may be developed internally by the organization or purchased from outside vendors. As noted above, this method is used by some of the organizations that we interviewed. Computerized systems may be particularly useful for large companies with substantial numbers of employees within the mentoring program, in which the task of carefully matching hundreds of mentors and protégés can become extremely cumbersome. Such an approach may be supported by the research that has consistently documented that mechanical (i.e. formal, statistical) prediction is superior to clinical (i.e. human) judgment.[33] However, the use of any computerized algorithm to match mentors and protégés will only be as good as the data that go into the system. The input of the appropriate characteristics and the weight given to each of them must be executed with care.

Case Study:
Citi

A major global financial services company had a new division CEO whose mission was to instill a mentoring culture where all leaders were willing to share their knowledge, expertise, and time with others to ensure a rewarding and enriching professional experience.

As a result, a mentoring program targeting high potentials was integrated into the division's overall leadership development framework. One key feature that made this program a standout was the matching process.

When the program was launched, there were 15 potential mentors who were part of the division's executive leadership team. In preparation for the matching process, the HR heads from each business line prepared a list of four potential protégés for the pool and a profile of information about each of them. The criteria for initial inclusion in this pool was that the individual was (a) identified as high potential; (b) no more than three levels below the pool of mentors; and (c) desiring a mentor.

At the matching meeting, each HR head presented the profile of each of the potential protégés, including their strengths, needs, and career aspirations. This information was garnered in part from their development plans and management profiles, similar to internal résumés. Once each potential protégé was presented, possible matches were discussed based on the strengths, experiences, and practical considerations (such as time zones) of the potential mentors.

Thus, each person at the meeting came to the table with knowledge of the potential mentor he/she represented and several potential protégés. This allowed for a robust and candid dialogue,

Continued

and confidence in the matches made that might not have existed through a questionnaire matching process. It took about four hours for the 15 mentors to be matched with one or two protégés from outside their own business. Each of the individuals not matched with a member of the executive committee was provided a mentor in their own business unit.

Action Plan:
Matching Mentors and Protégés

- Once the pool of mentors and protégés is determined (Action Plan for Chapter 3), the mentoring steering committee should discuss the goals of the program, the cultural expectations of the organization, and the resources available to determine a matching strategy.
- Determine what specific characteristics will be used for the match, and measure (or gather information) on those characteristics.
- If multiple characteristics will be used in matching, determine a weighting system.
- Determine if a computer algorithm will be used for the match; if so, put in place (in-house or through the use of consultant).
- If a computer algorithm will not be used, determine who will be responsible for making the matches.
- If mentor or protégé input will be used, determine how those individuals will garner information about potential partners (e.g., through written information, social function, or individual interviews).
- Determine a time frame for completing the matches and schedule all needed meetings/interviews/events.
- Decide how the match information will be communicated to the participants.
- If more potential mentors were recruited than actually needed, determine how to inform those not chosen of your decision.

Chapter 5

Training

A common recommendation in the field of organizational development is that individuals should be given adequate training and orientation when they are about to assume a new role, assignment, or job. Assuming a role in a formal mentoring program should be no exception. Training and preparatory activities can be an important component in a program's success. Training offers the opportunity to communicate program goals and expectations. It also helps prepare both the mentor and the protégé to handle their respective roles and responsibilities effectively. Additionally, training and orientation can be used to jump-start the building of the relationship, as well as provide the mentor and protégé with tools, behaviors, and skills that they can use to deal with unforeseen problems, conflicts, and obstacles. Ensuring that both parties are well equipped to participate in the mentoring program is key to the program's success – no amount of planning, structure, guidelines, matching procedures, check-ins, etc., will be helpful if both parties do not have the skills, abilities, confidence, and knowledge to be effective partners in the mentoring relationship.

In this chapter we discuss: (1) the evidence that training is necessary and can be helpful for a formal mentoring program; (2) developing training objectives; (3) suggestions for training content; (4) training delivery; and (5) post-training support and evaluation. Our focus is on the specifics needed for training associated with a formal mentoring program. Program administrators may also want to consult more general and/or comprehensive guides with regard to the overall training enterprise.[1] In the appendices we provide material that can be used to help develop training for the mentoring program. Appendix G is a sample mentoring training course outline, Appendix H is a sample training schedule, Appendix I is a sample experiential exercise for both mentors and protégés with an overview for trainers and complete role play material for the mentor exercise, and finally, Appendix J is a sample wrap-up activity. These materials may be modified for use as needed by the organization.

The Case for Training and Supporting Research Evidence

Trade publications regarding formal mentoring have long advocated training as part of a formal mentoring program. Recent research within workplace settings supports this suggestion in that both protégés and mentors appear to benefit from training. Training for mentors and for protégés has been associated with greater mentor commitment, greater understanding of the mentoring program, and perceptions of program effectiveness.[2] Training has also been positively associated with mentor and protégé reports of the amount of mentoring behavior received (e.g., psychosocial support).[3] Finally, research has shown that training effectiveness is associated with the benefit of helping the mentor meet generativity needs, meaning that the mentor is more likely to feel as if he or she is making a positive contribution toward the development of those more junior to him or herself when adequately prepared for the role.[4]

Training is common in mentoring programs designed for youth.[5] Research regarding other forms of mentoring such as that organized through Big Brothers/Big Sisters demonstrates a link between relationship quality and training. Mentors who receive preparatory training develop higher quality relationships than those who do not receive training. Training for mentors is also associated with mentor retention and beneficial protégé outcomes.

Thus, the research evidence from both workplace and youth mentoring literatures is relatively clear – when training is used to prepare participants for participating in formal mentoring programs, positive outcomes typically result.

Developing Training Objectives

In terms of the development of the training program, the organization should again first return to the objectives of the mentoring program. A "one-size fits all" approach to training is unlikely to be successful. As discussed further below, although some training is likely to be common across all types of formal mentoring programs, a significant portion of training should be developed that is based on and integrated with program objectives and goals. In order to do this, program designers should evaluate the program's objectives and determine what tasks, knowledges, skills, and abilities will be required of mentors and protégés, and then base the training program's objectives and content on those areas. For example, consider a mentoring program whose objective is to prepare a qualified pool of succession candidates for senior leadership positions. Since a large component of this program will focus on protégé skill development, it seems important that both mentors and protégés be taught skills and abilities that will help facilitate a learning relationship (e.g., how to give constructive feedback; how to learn from experience; how to create a development plan). Likewise, protégés may need to be oriented to the boundaries and limitations of the program.

In many instances, training objectives will be the same for protégés and mentors. For example, if formal mentoring is relatively new for the organization, or if participants have not participated in formal mentoring before, then both would need to "Understand What Mentoring Is and Is Not." However, other training objectives may be tailored to either the protégé or mentor, perhaps necessitating separate training programs. For example, new mentors may need training in how to "Give Direct, Constructive, and Helpful Feedback" whereas protégés may need training on "How to Accept Direct, Constructive, and Helpful Feedback." Below we provide some sample training objectives for mentors and for protégés.

Example: Sample Training Objectives	
For Mentors	**For Protégés**
• Understand what mentoring is and is not • Understand the roles, functions, and duties of a mentor • Understand the skills needed to be an effective mentor • Understand what to expect from your protégé • Be able to recognize and resolve potential mentoring problems and conflicts • Learn ways to structure, conduct, and sustain a valuable mentoring relationship • Increase comfort and confidence at being a mentor	• Understand what mentoring is and is not • Understand the roles, functions, and duties of a protégé • Understand the skills needed to be an effective protégé • Understand what to expect from your mentor • Understand what is expected of you • Be able to recognize and resolve potential mentoring problems and conflicts • Learn ways to structure, conduct, and sustain a valuable mentoring relationship • Understand how to best learn from experience

Potential Training Topics

Although benefits for training have been identified, there has been little direct research to suggest the specific topics and types of training that effectively facilitate and maintain high quality mentoring relationships. Based on our review of the mentoring and training literature, as well as our practical experience, we believe that a variety of topics can be included depending on the objectives and design of a formal mentoring program. Furthermore, we believe that it is helpful to think about training content in terms of different "layers," starting with basic foundational topics and progressing through more advanced and tailored issues.

The first layer of training content that we believe needs to be a part of any mentoring training includes basic, foundational topics that would be appropriate for any formal mentoring program regardless of its structure or design. Potential training topics for the first layer of training include defining mentoring, outlining the program's objectives, reviewing roles and responsibilities for the mentor and/or the protégé, outlining what protégés and mentors can and cannot expect, setting expectations and understanding the program's limitations, and introducing participants to problems typical of formal mentoring relationships. Throughout the training, mentors and protégés should be instructed to realize that they play the biggest role in determining the success of the relationship. These basic issues emerge as important in research. Data from one study suggested that what mentors would most like to see in training programs is more information regarding expectations and directions for the program. This included goals to work toward and suggestions regarding the process a mentor might use to identify how to best serve the needs of the protégé.[6] Given the nature of these training topics, it may be beneficial to have both protégés and mentors participate together in the training sessions. We recommend that when covering these and other mentoring training topics, a combination of discussion, activities, and lecture be used.[7]

The foundation and minimum training for any formal mentoring program should include the issues listed in the box below.

Basic Training for Mentors and Protégés

- Define mentoring
- Outline program objectives
- Review responsibilities of mentors and of protégés
- Review role of program staff
- Set expectations for what the program can and cannot do
- Establish relationships' structure and boundaries
- Describe potential relationship challenges
- Describe the structure of the formal mentoring program

The second layer of training also covers basic, foundational information, but varies from the first layer of training in that the information should be tailored to the needs, objectives, structure, and design of the organization's unique mentoring program. For example, if the purpose of the mentoring program is to promote diversity efforts, then training may include information on sensitivity to different gender and racial issues. As the structure and design of mentoring programs will vary across organizations, both protégés and mentors should be taught "how" to participate in the mentoring program, including topics such as: (1) how to use tools if applicable such as an on-line screening data-base; (2) specific information about how often pairs are required to meet; and (3) how progress will be monitored and evaluated. Specific issues covering distance learning should be discussed if the program requires mentor–protégé pairs who are located in disperse geographical locations. For programs designed to prepare a qualified succession pool for senior leadership positions, it may be helpful to instruct protégés and mentors that participation in the program does not constitute a guaranteed promotion. Again, as this represents foundational information, we believe this layer needs to be a part of any mentoring training program.

After securing the foundation, the third layer of training should focus on building specific skills and knowledge that protégés and mentors will need in order to develop and maintain a high quality mentoring relationship. Given that many of these skills transcend the mentoring program and thus may have been learned or screened through other means (e.g., leadership training; selection criteria for one's position or participation in the mentoring program), some organizations, particularly those with limited resources, may not need or may choose not to cover this information in-depth. For those that do, skills such as communicating clearly and with impact, listening actively and attentively, delivering direct and constructive feedback in a way that maintains the target's esteem, building trusting relationships through strong interpersonal skills, and managing and resolving conflicts can all be of benefit and ripe for training. Knowledge areas could include how to create a specific and actionable development plan, different tools, activities, and techniques for coaching and developing others, and the role of networks in aiding career progression. This layer of training may also include suggestions for building interpersonal comfort and trust with diverse others.

It is likely that in this third layer of training, certain topics may be more or less appropriate for either mentors or for protégés, necessitating separate training sessions. For example, for mentors, training on coaching and feedback skills could be extremely useful while, for protégés, the training may focus on how to use feedback and accept feedback with an open mind. Mentors may also benefit from instruction regarding role modeling and motivational techniques.[8] Having separate training sessions for mentors and for protégés allows them the opportunity to express their unique concerns. A combination of protégé-specific, mentor-specific, and joint training activities should be considered ideal. As many of the skill and knowledge areas taught at the third layer of training are behavior oriented, experiential activities, such as role-plays and demonstrations, should be utilized when possible.

Case Study:
Quest Diagnostics

Quest Diagnostics, Incorporated is a leading U.S. provider of diagnostic testing, information, and services that serves approximately 50% of all U.S. hospitals and physicians. Quest employs approximately 40,000 individuals, and is comprised of a distributed network of 35 regional laboratories, 150 rapid response laboratories, and over 2,200 patient service centers.

Quest's mentoring program goes by the acronym GENESIS, which stands for Growth, Engagement, Networking, Excellence, Satisfaction, Innovation, and Success. The main goal for this program is to help the company build the leadership pipeline. This includes a focus on identifying high potentials, developing leaders, fostering knowledge in a collaborative environment, and retaining highly skilled and talented people.

Quest Diagnostics has an extensive training session for both mentors and protégés. The sessions are held at the beginning and midway in the 12-month partnership. The Introductory session is a 3-4-hour workshop for the mentoring pairs after they have been matched. The training, designed by Leadership Technologies, is multi-faceted, including lecture (e.g., mentoring as a component of adult learning), the presentation of ground rules, coaching on communication, and video case studies demonstrating how to manage what can break down in relationships. There is also time allotted for the creation of a partnership learning plan, where goals for the relationship are articulated together.

The Advanced session is designed to focus on feedback and coaching with an emphasis on reinforcing skills and helping participants to more easily utilize these processes in their mentoring partnership.

The fourth, and final, layer of training should cover advanced issues that sometimes influence the success of close, organizational relationships. One such issue involves the challenges and obstacles that are likely to occur during the course of the mentoring relationship. While this information is to be introduced during the first layer of training (i.e., foundational information), and although the skills covered in the third layer of training can help, we believe more in-depth training and practice would be beneficial in helping participants resolve these concerns. Preparing mentors and protégés in advance with regard to what challenges they might encounter and providing strategies for dealing with them should be a component of training.

Like any relationship, interpersonal disagreements and misunderstandings may occur during the course of the mentoring relationship. For example, protégé accounts of interpersonal difficulties encountered during the course of mentoring relationship include tyrannical or manipulative behavior on the part of the mentor, mentors who lack technical or interpersonal skills, a mismatch in terms of values and personality, overprotection and paternalism by mentors, and neglect by the mentor. Negative experiences are not limited to the protégé, as mentors also report experiencing problems related to mentoring others. Those include a drain on time, difficulty dealing with protégés who have performance problems, protégés who are unwilling to learn, protégé deception and betrayal, and concerns regarding jealousy or favoritism.[9] We believe training should focus on discussing these issues in detail and providing participants a chance to role-play and work through sample situations that may arise.

Training Delivery

Depending on the resources within the organization, training may be conducted by in-house staff or contracted with an outside vendor. Most training professionals recommend that a variety of training methods be used that include lectures or presentations, experiential exercises, and group discussion activities. New technologies are also more commonly being implemented into training. For example, products that offer online mentoring training to mentors and protégés now have appeared on the market. This can permit a participant to be trained at a time that is convenient for him or her. Such methods may also be advantageous when program participants are geographically dispersed. However, given that mentoring revolves around interpersonal processes, training modes in which participants can interact also have distinct advantages. The use of technology such as video-conferencing (discussed in Chapter 6) may be helpful in this regard.

The sample training course illustrated in Appendix H is designed for a full one-day session. This is for illustrative purposes only. Each organization will need to determine the appropriate amount of time that can be invested into training based on the number of topics to be covered, how many layers of training to address, and available resources. One important issue to consider when determining the length of training is that mentors may be more sensitive to the demands on their time than protégés.[10] Mentors in particular need to understand how the time invested in training will be value added in order to gain their commitment and participation. Clear and open communication is key to making this happen.

Post-Training Support and Evaluation

A common and persistent finding from the training and development research literature is that often what is taught during training is not "transferred" back to the real-life work setting. That is, once a person returns to the job, the knowledge, skills, abilities, behaviors, etc., that he or she learned during training are not used or applied to their work. Understandably, this can result in relatively little return for the organization's investment in training.

For this reason, it is often recommended that organizations undertake activities to facilitate the trainee's use of skills and knowledge on the job. One such recommendation is to provide on-going support after completion of the training program. Ongoing support is particularly important for mentors and has been shown to increase program effectiveness.[11] In a study of mentors who had participated in a formal program, the mentors emphasized the need to support and share ideas with each other. Mentors can share their own best practices with other mentors and help each other problem solve.[12] Organizations can facilitate this dialogue by holding periodic "get-togethers" whereby mentors come together to discuss their experiences, outline challenges, seek advice from one another, and share best practices to help each other problem solve. Another approach utilized by one of the companies we interviewed was to ask mentors to occasionally speak to the executive mentoring committee that oversees the program about their challenges and experiences and to seek assistance. Protégés may also benefit from post-training support through similar strategies. For example, they could meet regularly with the program administrator in order to do a quick debrief on how the relationship is proceeding and to seek guidance and instruction on how to use what they have learned in training within the relationship.

Good to Know:
Ways to Provide Ongoing Support for Mentors

- Hold periodic meetings just for mentors to learn from each other
- Have program staff available
- Electronic discussion groups

It is important that the effectiveness of the training associated with the mentoring program receive its own evaluation. For example, data should be collected that helps determine how well the training prepared both mentors and protégés for their role. An examination of overall program evaluation criteria can also be used to help assess the effectiveness of the training (see Chapter 7). A detailed discussed of training evaluation is beyond the scope of this book. Interested readers are again referred to existing resources for more information.[13]

Lessons Learned

- Give the protégé and mentor more tools and aids to help them make the most of the relationship.
- Find ways to encourage a sense of community among protégés through networking, that they can take with them as they progress into more senior levels of leadership.

Action Plan:
Training

- Determine the resources available to devote to training in terms of cost (e.g., for training materials) and time (for preparation as well as mentor, protégé, and trainer time away from work).
- Given the resources at your disposal, clearly state (in writing) your training objectives and determine how many layers of training would best suit your needs.
- Make an outline of the topics and specifics to be covered in the first layer of training (e.g., foundational topics such as objectives, roles, expectations). Create any needed presentation slides.
- Make an outline of the topics and specifics to be covered in the second layer of training (e.g., topics specific to your organization and the goals of your mentoring program). Create any needed presentation slides and practice activities.
- If including layer three training topics (knowledge and skill development), determine the specific knowledge and skills to be covered for mentors and for protégés. Determine if this will be done in separate training sessions. Create or find relevant experiential exercises and create any needed presentation slides.
- If including layer four training topics (more in-depth issues, like relationship challenges), determine what will be covered for mentors and for protégés. Determine if this will be done in separate training sessions. Create or find relevant experiential exercises and create any needed presentation slides.
- Do a "dry run" of the training sessions, possibly with the mentoring steering committee, to work out any problematic issues.
- Create a training evaluation strategy and any forms or materials to be used to evaluate the training program.
- Determine whether all participants will take part in one big training session or if there will be several for them to choose from. This may depend on the size of the program and the flexibility of schedules.
- Schedule and conduct training.
- Evaluate training and determine if improvements should be made.

Chapter 6

Mentoring Structure and Processes

Organizations face many choices that must be made when deciding on a structure for the mentoring process. Most formal mentoring programs provide some degree of procedures, control, and oversight covering issues such as creating a relationship, defining goals, meeting frequency, and the duration of the mentoring relationship. Structure is important to the extent that it facilitates mentor–protégé relationship building and helps the organization maximize its resources through a consistent and standardized approach to mentoring. Creating a structure for the mentoring relationship should serve the purpose of providing individuals with the tools needed to develop a successful alliance, not to apply a rigid formula for success. A mentoring relationship is like any other relationship – it is best negotiated by the actual relationship partners. In addition, corporate level strategy should precede any decisions regarding mentoring structure and processes (see Chapter 2). That is, decisions regarding structure should be driven by the overall purpose and objectives of the program.

In this chapter, we cover the issues that need to be considered when developing structural guidelines for the mentoring program. The six issues addressed include: (1) determining confidentiality standards; (2) expectations for the relationship; (3) meeting frequency and method; (4) relationship duration; (5) guiding protégé career development; and (6) planned activities.

Confidentiality Standards

Trust is thought to be an essential component of mentoring relationships. Mentoring works best when the protégé can feel comfortable with the mentor and be able to divulge information that may be sensitive. Thus, it is key to make sure that all parties are aware of what the standards are in terms of confidentiality and the importance of maintaining the standards. Several factors that need to be taken into consideration are included in the box below.

Mentoring Program Confidentiality Considerations

- Will protégés be provided with an assurance of confidentiality or will the mentor be asked to provide feedback to others regarding the protégé?
- If others are to be provided feedback on the protégé, who will be informed, what is the data to be used for, and how will they keep it in confidence?
- Will the protégé's supervisor be involved and if so how?; what is the role of the supervisor?
- Will the personal experience of the mentor that is shared with the protégé be kept in confidence?
- Even if confidentiality is highly enforced, under what conditions will it be permissible to share information with others (e.g., ethical breaches; unlawful activity)?
- How will confidence be assured when a protégé or mentor needs to approach a third party to seek relationship guidance and advice?

Although on the surface it may appear most desirable to ensure complete confidentiality in order to encourage open and honest sharing of information and feedback (and certainly this will apply to many programs), there are instances where it may be appropriate to share feedback with certain other individuals. Again, this would depend upon the goals of the program and the climate and culture of the organization. For example, if the goal of a program is to both identify and prepare high-potential managers for senior-level executive positions, it may be in the best interest of the organization and the protégé for the mentor to share his or her assessment of the protégé's experience, lessons learned, accomplishments, and developmental progress to an executive committee charged with overseeing the selection of executives. A protégé who creates a career development plan (see later in this chapter) may wish to share the plan with his or her supervisor and garner the supervisor's support for the plan.

Regardless of which decisions are made with respect to confidentiality, the following steps need to be taken for any program: (1) clear standards need to be developed regarding what information is and is not to be shared; (2) clear standards need to be developed regarding to whom and not to whom should this information be shared; (3) these standards need to be communicated clearly to all participants; and (4) consistent application of these standards must be monitored and enforced. A single serious deviation from confidentiality standards can irrevocably damage the reputation and credibility of the best-designed mentoring program.

Stating, Sharing, and Negotiating Expectations for the Relationship

Mentors and protégés need to set expectations, goals, and boundary conditions for their relationships. The organization can facilitate this process by encouraging the participants to create a mentoring plan that maps out activities, resources, and criteria for success. As discussed further below, this may include a mentoring agreement that outlines the mentor's and protégé's expectations and vision for the relationship. Training can be a good mechanism for facilitating this process (see Chapter 5) and be integrated with the purposes of the program.

Setting goals is an important part of the mentorship structure. Research shows that taking part in a goal-setting process with the mentor relates to protégé satisfaction.[1] This is not surprising when considering the highly robust findings in the organizational behavior literature regarding the effectiveness of goal-setting for producing positive results. Higher performance consistently results from goals that are challenging, achievable, and specific (rather than easy or general goals). Furthermore, stronger performance is achieved when the individual accepts the goal and receives feedback about his or her progress toward that goal.[2] Accordingly, a formal mentoring intervention should result in more positive outcomes to the extent that the mentor and protégé set mutually agreed upon specific, clear, and achievable goals.

Expectations are a part of all social relationships and the development of realistic expectations at the onset of the relationship can help avoid potential problems that could occur later.[3] Expectations evolve over time and experience, but individuals often begin a relationship with standard expectations that fit their preconceived ideas about what the relationship should be like. The term "mentoring" itself may have certain connotations associated with it that the mentoring partners bring into the relationship. Individuals may have developed their own understanding of what a "mentor" or "protégé" is prior to entering into a relationship, from which expectations are created before even meeting the actual mentoring partner. To the degree that the individual characteristics of the mentoring partner are not consistent with that understanding, the relationship may get off to a rocky start. If the pair addresses those expectancies and shapes new ones together, it can pave the way toward the development of an effective mentoring partnership.

Boundary setting is also an important consideration in negotiating the terms of the relationship.[4] The mentoring partners should have a discussion regarding what behaviors and interactions are and are not acceptable to them. Mentoring relationships can include interactions at settings inside the office, social settings, and at offsite locations that involve professional conferences and client travel. The mentoring pair should be encouraged to discuss issues such as the acceptability of phone calls (at home or at work), scheduled meetings versus unscheduled visits, socializing after work or at offsite events, acceptable meeting locations, etc. Individuals vary with regard to the extent that boundary spanning is deemed appropriate and comfortable. Consideration should also be given to any subject matter that may be considered off limits. For example, while the pair may agree that the topic of work–life balance challenges is appropriate, a discussion of marital problems is not. Opening a dialogue regarding these kinds of issues at the beginning of the relationship can help avoid misunderstandings and reduce role uncertainty. It also goes without saying that relationships that become romantic or sexual compromise the integrity of the mentoring relationship and the formal mentoring program.

Goals, expectations, and boundaries can be established through the use of a mentoring agreement. What is a mentoring agreement? A mentoring agreement is a common understanding between the protégé and the mentor as to the structural parameters of the mentoring relationship. Why have a mentoring agreement? The mentoring agreement serves several important purposes:

- It helps to anticipate and prevent potential obstacles that can occur during the course of the relationship.
- It helps to clarify mutual expectations and desired outcomes from the mentoring relationship.
- It serves as the foundation from which to determine the progress and the success of a mentoring relationship.

We stress that a mentoring agreement is not necessarily intended as a formal, written, contractual document. It is merely a framework for coming to a mutual understanding between the mentor and the protégé as to how the relationship will unfold. A template for structuring a mentoring agreement and a sample agreement that has been completed are provided in Appendix K.

Lessons Learned – Case Summary

Encourage Collaboration and Personal Contact

One company noted that having a face-to-face interaction at the outset of the program/training, and having the protégé and mentor work together to create a plan of action, was important to get the relationship moving forward. In fact, it was observed that those dyads that missed the initial orientation and did their make-up session without having personal connection (via web-based training) did not find the session as valuable and had a harder time getting going in their relationship.

Meeting Frequency and Mode of Contact

Other components to address when structuring the formal mentoring relationship are how often protégés and mentors should meet (interaction frequency) and the method for meeting (e.g., face-to-face contact or through telecommunications).

Meeting Frequency

With regard to meeting frequency, reviews of organizational practices suggest that organizations vary in how often, if at all, they require their mentors and employees to meet.[5] The most common recommendation was monthly interaction, with weekly meetings coming in second.

Research shows that having some guidelines in place is beneficial. For example, protégés in programs that provided guidelines for the frequency of meetings reported that the mentoring program was more effective than did protégés who were in programs with no guidelines.[6] Research also suggests that positive outcomes result from regular interaction frequency. Data from certified public accountants in formal mentoring programs indicated that protégés were more satisfied with their mentor when they had regular meetings.[7] Research from the formal mentoring youth arena also stresses regular contact.[8]

What is less clear is what should be the recommended amount of interaction. Data from formal mentoring programs have shown that meeting frequency is associated with psychosocial and career support, protégé work motivation, and protégé organizational commitment, which suggests that the greater the interaction, the more the benefits realized.[9] Similarly, in a study of a formal mentoring program for junior faculty, the actual amount of time the protégé and mentor spent together in person related to more favorable evaluations of the program, higher relationship quality, and more help from the mentor in meeting the protégé's goals.[10] However, given that concerns regarding time drain is the most common worry of mentors in terms of participating in formal programs, recommending more frequent interactions is often not a practical guideline.

It is recommended that discussion between the mentor and protégé regarding expectations and needs, as noted above, dictate meeting frequency. However, the organization should consider implementing some type of minimum guideline as a way of encouraging meetings between participants. Having guidelines is a signal of a well-organized and planned formal mentoring program in general. One additional recommendation to mentors and protégés may be to advise them to try and establish a schedule that is consistent. For example, the pair can commit to meeting for lunch every other

Tuesday. Just as important as setting the meeting is keeping it. It can be easy to allow "regular" work duties to take precedence when scheduling conflicts arise. However, canceling meetings risks sending a message that mentoring and the other mentoring partner are not important or a high priority, thus damaging the relationship.

Case Study:
Weyerhaeuser Company

Weyerhaeuser Company is an international forest products company employing approximately 37,900 individuals. Weyerhaeuser is ranked in the Fortune 200, and has annual net sales of $16.3 billion. As a company with stated values of diversity, development, and teamwork, Weyerhaeuser strongly supports mentoring as a key part of their retention strategy and has for many years. Company-supported mentoring has evolved over the years, however, to better fit the organization's culture. As Effenus Henderson, Chief Diversity Officer, explains "We realized we had to loosen up the structure and really tailor it to what the mentees need."

Weyerhaeuser found that by providing information to employees about mentoring through a website, a handbook, and an optional presentation, employees can manage expectations of what might be derived from a mentoring relationship. They allow protégés to either choose their own mentor or work with a manager or employee support network to locate a mentor. Suggested guidelines for the structure of the relationship are provided – for example, meeting approximately once per month to once per quarter, communicating regularly over email, and signing an agreement to manage expectations at the start of the relationship – but Henderson emphasizes that they take "no real cookie cutter approach to mentoring – it has to meet the needs of both partners."

Mode of Contact

Industry reports suggest that about half of formal mentoring programs allow for both face-to-face and distance relationships, with a little less than the other half focusing mainly on face-to-face relationships. The most widely reported technology used for non face-to-face communication was telephone and email (90% and 80% respectively), with the Internet/Intranet, faxes, and video-conferences used less frequently.[11] Research from program users, the mentors and the protégés, show that face-to-face contact is preferred.[12]

On the other hand, recent technological advancements have made non-face-to-face communication easier and more common. For example, as high-speed internet services have become more common world-wide, it is possible for video-conferencing to enable personal contact from many disparate geographic locations (e.g., one of this book's authors once conducted a coaching and feedback session via video-conferencing from the U.S. to a participant in China). The relatively cheap availability of web cameras makes this form of communication more possible and potentially more common in the future. In recent years the practice of "e-mentoring" has gained in popularity as well. This type of mentoring relies primarily on email communications as the basis for information, feedback, and guidance exchange. These alternative forms of contact have their obvious advantages, such as encouraging mentoring relationships across geographic locations and maximizing resource utilization. For example, such modes of contact can be a valuable tool for mentoring relationships that involve employees on an international assignment. There are disadvantages that the organization should consider as well, such as increased potential for miscommunication and misunderstandings, possible discomfort with sharing personal information over phone or data lines, and technological problems.

Given the relative newness of these practices, there is little research to evaluate their effectiveness as applied to the mentoring area; hence, there are few substantive recommendations we can offer. However, because of the importance of personal bonding for mentoring relationships to flourish, we recommend that in cases in which distance relationships are necessary, every effort be made to at least initiate the relationship through face-to-face contact to facilitate early relationship building. Regardless of organizational suggestions and/or policy, in order to avoid misunderstandings it is critical that the frequency and mode of contact be specified and agreed upon by the mentor and protégé.

Case Study:
Limited Brands

Limited Brands is a leading provider of women's intimate apparel, beauty and personal care products, with more than 2,900 stores employing nearly 100,000 associates. Its brands include Victoria's Secret, PINK, La Senza, Bath & Body Works, C.O. Bigelow, Henri Bendel and The White Barn Candle Company, generating more than $10 billion in sales in 2007. Limited Brands uses a practical and user-friendly mentoring program to provide developmental opportunities for high potential associates.

As noted by Dennis Armstrong, Senior Vice President of Talent and Organizational Effectiveness, Limited Brands had debated the design and development of a formal mentoring program over several years. Dennis and his team determined there was interest in mentoring which they wanted to support, but did not want to elevate expectations to a point that they could not support. As a result, they developed guides for mentors and protégés that defined reasonable expectations for each and provided a simple process to maximize benefits from the relationship for both parties. They introduced structure to the program by using the company's Organizational Leadership Review Process to formally identify potential protégés. Dennis and the team then established guiding principles to ensure shared responsibility among the four key roles: the HR Partner, protégé, the protégé's direct manager, and the mentor.

Process steps included:

- Contacting the protégé's HR leader and direct manager in order to gain a sense of the protégé's developmental opportunities and needs.
- Providing the protégé with the opportunity to suggest the names of potential mentors.
- Providing the protégé and mentor with a simple guide that explained the purpose of the relationship and their roles and responsibilities.

The program was able to retain a significant degree of flexibility for the following reasons:

- Matching between mentors and protégés was more collegial and less prescriptive.

Continued

- Frequency or method of meetings between the mentoring pair was left up to the participants.
- The launch of the guide as a suggested process did not include elaborate training, kick-off, or orientation sessions.
- Although best practice guidelines were provided, specific activities or outputs from the relationship (e.g., development plans) were not required.

By balancing the formal and informal aspects of its program, Limited Brands' leaders believe it is better able to manage participants' expectations as to what to gain from the program. In addition, this approach allows for more flexibility for participants to determine how they manage the relationships, thus better meeting their needs. And finally, this approach relies more on the participants' commitment to make it work, and is a better fit for the company's culture.

From a success standpoint, Limited Brands' leaders note that several participants have been promoted and moved on to different jobs within the company, and almost all participants report feeling more valued, appreciated, and connected to the company.

Relationship Duration

Mentoring relationships are thought to have some form of a beginning, middle, and end to them. The beginning phase may generally consist of rapport building and the development of mutual trust. If such bonding does not occur, the relationship may essentially end there. That is why it is vital that the organization think carefully regarding its matching process (see Chapter 4). If some degree of natural bonding occurs, then the participants may focus on achieving the objectives of the relationship. At the end of the contracted period the participants may choose to continue the relationship on an informal basis, redefine the relationship, or end it altogether.

Informal mentoring relationships are thought to last approximately 5–6 years. Formal mentoring relationships are contracted for a much shorter period. The timing of the stages of relationship development has been given little attention in the formal mentoring research literature. We do know that relationship duration makes a difference in the outcomes realized.[13] In fact, there is some evidence that the longer the formal relationship lasts, the more it meets the quality and level of outcomes realized as that of informal mentoring relationships. We also know that there is a great degree of variability across companies regarding the recommended length of the relationships. Companies have reported having formal mentoring relationships last as short as three months to as long as three years.[14]

No research is available that has directly investigated differences between workplace formal programs of varying durations (e.g., comparisons of programs contracted for 3 months versus 6 months versus 12 months). However, relationship duration has demonstrated small but significant relationships with protégé career commitment, organizational commitment, organizational-based self-esteem, perceptions of justice, and reduced intention to quit, which suggests that relationships longer in duration achieve greater protégé benefits than those shorter in duration. Research from the youth mentoring literature also yields insight into this issue, suggesting that the longer the relationship, the better the outcomes. Program evaluations suggest that it takes around six months for mentors and protégés to establish a relationship that can have impact. Relationships of shorter duration result in no significant positive changes.[15] This is not surprising given that theory regarding informal mentoring relationships suggests most relationships last 5–6 years before terminating or evolving into one of peers.[16]

One approach to consider is to allow the participants to decide how long the relationship should last. However, one benefit to having a specific contracted duration for the relationship may be that it motivates the participants to focus energy to accomplish goals within a specified timeframe. Specified relationship duration also makes it easier for the organization to systematically monitor and evaluate the effectiveness of mentoring relationships (see Chapter 7). As noted previously, the participants can choose to continue their relationship beyond its contractual boundary or maintain periodic contact.

An organization should consider its developmental culture and the goals of the mentoring program when determining how long a mentoring relationship should last (e.g., a mentoring program focused on providing job/technical skills to new hires may be shorter in length than a program designed to increase females' exposure to senior leadership positions). However, based on the research evidence at hand we recommend that six months be the minimum considered.

Guiding Protégé Career Development

From the organization's perspective, as discussed in Chapter 2, mentoring works best when it is integrated with other Human Resource development systems such as career development programs. For the protégé, the mentoring relationship is a unique opportunity to focus on his or her career development and can be a key element of an overall career plan. Done with purpose and planning, mentoring should be much more than meeting over lunch or coffee for brief exchanges of information. The pair should develop a specific, actionable agenda with working timelines to completion. Two tools that can be used to help facilitate the protégé career development process within a mentoring relationship are a protégé career planning form and a mentoring action plan. Appendix L contains a career planning form and a sample completed form. Appendix M includes materials related to the mentoring action plan. Working through these exercises will help protégés determine what goals they want to achieve and how their mentors can help facilitate the process.

In working through a career development plan, it is helpful to remember that to a great extent the mentoring process should be protégé driven. That is, the protégé should provide input for goals and ground rules for the relationship.[17] However, while mentors should be focused on the protégés' interests and needs, they should also be given some leeway in determining how they can best assist protégés. Some protégés may feel as though they are imposing upon the mentor and be hesitant to make contact for fear of infringing too much on the mentor's time. Successful mentors engage in proactive behaviors such as initiating regular contact, ensuring that meetings are scheduled, and reviewing protégé progress toward goal completion.[18]

Planned Activities

The topic of training was discussed in depth in Chapter 5. In addition to training, other types of planned activities may be built into the overall structure of the formal mentoring program. For example, "kick-off" social events designed to get all mentors and protégés together is a common activity used by many programs. This permits all of the participants to begin to bond and become acquainted. Other potential planned events include panel discussions with previous protégés and/or experienced mentors, focus groups to review successes and problems, periodic sponsored lunches for all participants, and "graduation" events at the end of the program.

Action Plan:
Mentoring Structure and Processes

- Make decisions about the level of confidentiality required of the mentors and protégés; communicate this to them and decide if it should be part of a written mentoring agreement. If it is determined that mentors will share information on protégés to supervisors/organizational leaders, the nature of the information that will be shared should be clarified to all parties.
- Decide whether a mentoring agreement will be used and design the template of an agreement to include information to guide goal setting, boundary setting, and expectations.
- Determine whether the meeting frequency guidelines will be mandated by the committee, only suggested by the committee, or fully determined by the pairs. Communicate this to the pairs.
- Determine if the mode of conduct will be only in person, or in person combined with phone and/or electronic communication, or if this will be decided by the pairs. Communicate this to the pairs.
- Determine whether the length of the relationships will be set by the mentoring committee or set by individual pairs; if by committee, decide on the length and communicate this to the pairs.
- Communicate to the pairs what the expected roles are of protégés and mentors for driving the process.
- Decide if a protégé development plan will be used by the pair and, if so, design a template to include whatever components make sense for the goals of the program.
- Decide on the type of planned activities to be included in the program.

Chapter 7

Monitoring and Program Evaluation

In order to determine whether or not a mentoring program is achieving the business goals and objectives it was designed to achieve, it is imperative that companies create and implement a monitoring and evaluation process as part of their programs. Monitoring processes can help gauge problems early enough to be corrected quickly, and evaluation procedures can help establish the effectiveness of a formal mentoring program. The importance of evaluation and monitoring cannot be over-stated, especially considering that, to date, research tends to indicate that formal mentoring relationships are less effective than are informal mentorships (but better than no mentoring).[1] In today's increasingly competitive business environment, where resources are often stretched and limited, the mentoring program's survival and viability depend on it demonstrating a sound return on investment. Following the steps outlined in previous chapters can help organizations facilitate high quality mentoring relationships where learning and growth take place. Monitoring and evaluation are the way to translate that learning and growth into demonstrable value-added business results.

As has been emphasized throughout this book, the steps and measures that are used to monitor and evaluate the program should flow directly from its stated goals as well as the overall company culture. For example, as formal mentoring programs are often designed to enhance newcomer socialization or retain talent rather than to increase promotion rates and salaries, a relevant measure may be the number of protégés who remain with the company for five or more years, but not how much their salaries rise (or drop) during that time period. As noted in Chapter 1, outcome criteria and plans to evaluate the program should be created and in place before the first mentoring relationship is formed.

In this chapter we provide information concerning ways in which to monitor and evaluate formal mentoring programs. Monitoring and evaluation allow you to support and strengthen individual relationships and to also gain insight into ways to improve the overall effectiveness of the mentoring program. The focus of monitoring is at the level of the individual relationships while evaluation is focused on the program as a whole.

Monitoring

Monitoring serves several purposes. It helps to make sure that the participants are meeting regularly and that they are making progress toward their goals. Furthermore, monitoring serves the purpose of identifying relationships that are "in trouble" and may need to be repaired or be terminated. Another benefit of monitoring is that periodic check-ins with the participants help convey support for the program as a whole. Research shows that both mentors and protégés believe that monitoring is essential for effective formal programs. Moreover, programs that include ongoing facilitation of the mentoring relationship have been shown to lead to greater gains in positive job attitudes (e.g., job satisfaction) than programs without facilitation.[2] Research has also shown that perceived accountability (from the perspective of protégés) has been associated with fewer accounts of mentor manipulation/cynicism and role indifference. Accountability perceptions have also been associated with fewer perceived mismatched pairs and fewer reports of mentors lacking expertise.[3] Thus, ample research supports the need for the monitoring process.

In designing its monitoring process, the organization needs to take three issues into consideration: (1) the *frequency* of monitoring; (2) the *method* of monitoring; (3) and the *content* of what is to be monitored.

Frequency of Monitoring

Check-ups may occur weekly, monthly, quarterly, or semi-annually. More frequent check-ups early in the relationship probably work best, and once the relationship is established, check-ups can be done with longer intervals in between. More frequent check-ups might also be wise when a new mentoring program is just getting off the ground and the organization is working out the kinks. As a guideline, consider contacting the pair within the first two weeks of the match to make sure the relationship has started off well.

Method of Collecting Data

There are several choices available in terms of the method used to collect monitoring data. For example, the program administrator may choose to send out short surveys to participants. In other cases, face-to-face meetings may be conducted or participants may be queried via phone contact. Group meetings may also be helpful for monitoring the program in general. However, if group meetings are used, participants also need to be given the opportunity to provide information that may be considered of a sensitive nature in a confidential format (e.g., one-on-one meeting with the program administrator).

Content of the Monitoring

Topics that can be covered in the review include what is working with the mentoring relationship, what are the problems, what is causing those problems, and suggestions for how things might be improved. In the box below we provide several sample questions that can be used. The organization may want to develop a unique set of questions for mentors and for protégés.

Sample Monitoring Questions (Protégé Perspective)

- How often are you and your mentor meeting?
- Does your mentor appear committed to the mentoring process? In what way?
- How effective is the communication between you and your mentor?
- Do you feel that your mentoring needs are being addressed? In what ways?
- Are there any problems occurring within the relationship? Please explain.

Continued

- What is going well about your relationship?
- What progress have you made toward your goals for the relationship?
- Is there any way in which the program can help improve your mentoring experience? How?

Undoubtedly, monitoring will sometimes identify matches that are not working as well as desired. In such circumstances, organizations need to have a plan in place for what to do. If monitoring reveals that the relationship is not working out, then a clear plan of action can be created in order to try to improve the relationship. If, however, continued corrective actions are unsuccessful, it is recommended that organizations allow mentors and protégés to end relationships without repercussion. Procedures need to be developed in the planning stages of the program that help participants terminate their relationships if necessary. Waiting until a problem occurs is not recommended. The program administrator may have the role of facilitating this process. The procedures and processes in place should be communicated to both mentors and protégés during orientation or training.

Sample Monitoring Questions (Mentor Perspective)

- How often do you and your protégé meet?
- Does your protégé appear committed to the mentoring process? In what way?
- How effective is the communication between you and your protégé?
- Do you feel that you are making progress in helping your protégé address the developmental goals? Why or why not?
- Are there any problems occurring within the relationship? What are these?
- What is going well about your relationship?
- Is there any way in which the program can help improve your mentoring experience? How?

Even in relationships that are generally effective, there may be times in which the participants experience frustration and difficulty. For example, there could be a conflict over a particular issue and participants' efforts to resolve the conflict have been unsuccessful, despite the fact that overall the relationship has been progressing smoothly. The program administrator needs the skills to be able to distinguish the difference between temporary setbacks versus a relationship that is simply not working. Frequent monitoring can catch these temporary setbacks soon enough that they do not become significant, exaggerated problems that are more difficult to resolve.

The best monitoring practice is also one that tracks relationship data across time to see how relationships are growing and evolving. This information can be helpful in terms of making adjustments to training, support, suggested relationship duration, etc. Short surveys that gather numerical rankings can be a useful tool for quantitatively identifying trends, improvement opportunities, and areas of progress over time.

Good to Know:
Problems to Be on the "Look Out" for in Mentoring Relationships

- Meetings are not occurring
- Mentor/protégé claims that s/he is being ignored/ neglected by the other
- Mentor feels overwhelmed by the time commitment
- Mentor/protégé seem to lack interest

Program Evaluation

As described earlier, evaluation of any organizational intervention is an important step in determining its ultimate value to the organization. As is the case with monitoring, evaluation of a formal mentoring program serves several purposes. First, it provides a systematic process to help determine if the program is meeting its stated goals and objectives. Second, it can help gauge whether the program is meeting its goals in a cost-effective manner. Third, it helps to identify possible areas for improvement or change to certain aspects of the program (e.g., matching process; meeting frequency). Fourth, along with monitoring, evaluation helps to ensure that participants have positive attitudes toward the program and are using it effectively. Fifth, done effectively (and assuming positive results), results from the evaluation can help justify the continued existence of the program and build commitment from key organizational decision makers. Finally, done to scientific standards, evaluation can help provide valid data that the professional community can use to provide further research and investigation into formal mentoring programs.

Good to Know:
How Program Evaluation Data Can be Used

- Produce data to support and promote the program to stakeholders
- Verify that you are achieving the goals you set out to achieve

- Examine and describe the program for duplication in other parts of the organization
- Determine ways in which the existing program can be improved

---

In determining how best to design an evaluation process for a mentoring program, there are several issues that need to be considered. These issues include *what* factors and variables will be measured, *how* those factors and variables will be measured, *who* will provide information on the factors and variables, *when* will the results be measured, and in *what* manner will results be compared and evaluated.

What to Measure

A wide range of factors and variables may be considered as part of a program evaluation. Again, the choice of what to measure will depend on the program's objectives, and will partly determine the methods used for data collection (e.g., surveys for reaction measures vs. observation to assess behavioral change). As discussed in Chapter 1, when setting the program's objectives it is important to make them specific and measurable. Having done that, the process of selecting criteria for evaluation becomes more straightforward. Sample evaluation materials are included in Appendices N and O.

We propose considering possible evaluation measures and criteria from three different perspectives. First, evaluation measures can be either qualitative and/or quantitative in nature. Second, evaluation measures can vary as to whether they are targeted toward the individual person or the organization as a whole. Third, evaluation measures can vary according to the degree they reflect one or more of Kirkpatrick's four levels of measurement: (1) *reactions* to the training; (2) *learning* that resulted from the training; (3) *behavior* or *performance* change; and (4) business *results* for the organization.[4] These are elaborated further below. Overall, it is our recommendation that in order to provide a more robust, comprehensive evaluation, the organization try to include as many of these elements as possible in its selection of evaluation criteria, given resource constraints and the program's goals.

Qualitative vs. Quantitative Measures

Qualitative measures, by definition, are indices that focus on describing or categorizing the characteristics or qualities of some variable of interest. These are data that can easily be observed, yet generally are not assessed numerically in terms of higher or lower values. Quantitative measures, on the other hand, are focused on measuring amount and quantity, and are thus numerically-based. For example, a qualitative evaluation of a painting may indicate that it contains blue and red as predominant colors, is surrealistic in nature, and has heavily-emphasized brush strokes. A quantitative analysis of that same painting would indicate that it is 20 inches wide by 12 inches tall and weighs 3 pounds, costing $5,000 (if one is so talented).

Applied to the mentoring area, possible qualitative measures would be participants' verbal or written comments about things that worked well in the program, things that did not work well, ideas on what to improve in the mentoring program, and how much they believed they learned during the relationship. To evaluate qualitative data many researchers will look for themes and often group similar responses, which allows them to tally how frequently a particular response was given (e.g., 20 out of 32 protégés indicate they gained more self-confidence through their mentoring relationship). This method can make qualitative data more numerical in nature. Possible quantitative measures of mentoring program success could be how many meetings took place between a mentor and protégé, ratings of their satisfaction with the program, income levels of protégés, and retention statistics.

Individual vs. Organizational Measures

Individual-level variables are those measures that are focused on the individual participants in the mentoring program. Examples include the protégé's satisfaction with his or her mentor, the mentor's satisfaction with his or her protégé, the protégé's job attitudes, and the protégé's level of performance improvement. Organizational variables, on the other hand, focus on company-wide measures that cut across multiple individuals. Applied to formal mentoring programs, examples could include turnover/retention rates for protégés, culture and climate measures (e.g., overall job satisfaction), and financial indicators (e.g., money saved via increased retention).

Levels of Measurement

Finally, evaluation measures, according to Kirkpatrick, can focus on participants' reactions, learning, and behavior/performance change, and overall company results. By definition these levels can include both qualitative and quantitative measures, as well as individual and organizational variables.

- *Reaction measures* typically have the participant/target directly self-report their evaluation of the program – Were they satisfied? Did they like it? Was it relevant to their work? Were they happy with the activities? These measures are usually best obtained immediately or soon following an event. It is highly recommended that a formal mentoring program make use of reaction measures as they can help identify areas for improvement and they may help explain other results (e.g., whether or not learning took place may be related to participants' reactions to the program).

- *Learning measures* involve an assessment of how much actual learning occurred during the mentoring program. For example, a protégé in a socialization program could be tested on his or her knowledge of the organization's structure, or participants in training could be tested on whether they learned the training materials sufficiently. A common method for gauging learning is to administer a test of participants' knowledge before and after the mentoring program (or any instructional intervention). Again, it is recommended to measure one's learning soon after the intervention when the data is fresh on people's minds, although some organizations may wish to also test at a later date to gauge how much information was retained over time.
- The next level of measurement involves *behavior* or *performance change*. Here, the organization is interested in whether or not the skills, knowledge, or experience that the participant gained translated into actual behavior change. Examples could be an improvement in one's communication skills, the protégé's increased sales performance, or holding more frequent coaching sessions with one's employees. This level of measurement is key in determining whether the "transfer of training" problem that plagues many training and development activities is also an issue within a company's mentoring program.
- *Business results* involve organizational-level measures of success. It is helpful to think of this level in terms of "bottom-line" results – Did the organization's revenues increase? Were costs reduced? Did turnover drop? Has production increased substantially? While these results are not difficult to measure, unless a strong research design is used, the difficulty with using this level of measurement is determining whether or not the improved business results were *due to* the mentoring program and not some other event (e.g., economic policies; change in consumer spending; new product introduction). We recommend that if this level of measurement is used in evaluating a formal mentoring program, then (1) the measures need to be strongly and logically linked to the program's goals (e.g., a program designed to improve employee retention should not be expected to be measured by increases in sales performance); and (2) careful research design methodology be used that takes into account the impact of other factors that could influence results (see below).

Example Evaluation Measures

	Individual	Organizational
Reaction	• Satisfaction with the mentoring relationship[qq] • Perceived usefulness of the relationship[qq] • Degree to which progress is being made toward goals[qq] • Written comments about what worked well, not well, and what needs to be improved[q]	Not applicable
Learning	• Improvement between pre-test and post-test on a measure of knowledge • Performing a task or activity more effectively immediately after training[qq] • Understanding a greater number of influence tactics[qq] • Observed performance on a simulated task immediately after training[qq]	Not applicable
Behavior/ Performance	• Improved job performance • Improved 360-degree feedback ratings • Higher performance appraisal ratings • Number of meetings that took place between the mentor and protégé	• Number of protégés who have made improvements in performance appraisal ratings • Number of protégés who have seen 360-degree feedback improvements

	• Self-reports of how often a protégé is performing an activity[q] • Mentors willing to continue to participate in the program	• Number of mentors volunteering to participate in the next mentoring program
Results	• Increased sales performance • Getting tasks done more quickly[qq] • Saving money for the company • Income level	• Retention/turnover statistics • Revenue • Climate and culture indices • Costs

Note: Measures noted with a single 'q' represent qualitative measures; measures noted with a double 'qq' represent measures that can be either qualitative or quantitative; all other measures are quantitative.

How to Measure

There are many tools a company can use to measure results. Some tools are more or less appropriate for assessing certain measures that were described above. One assessment tool is the *one-on-one interview*, whereby the evaluator (e.g., program administrator) will meet individually with each program participant to gather his or her comments and thoughts about the program. This approach can provide rich, comprehensive data as the interviewer can follow-up and probe in depth on unclear responses or important issues. Most interviews focus on gathering qualitative data at the individual level, although gathering participants' quantitative ratings on multiple factors is possible as well (i.e., the interviewer reads an evaluative item [e.g., Rate your satisfaction with your mentor] and the participant rates it on a 1–5 scale [1 = Unsatisfied; 5 = Highly Satisfied]). Typically, reaction and/or self-reported learning and behavior change data are gathered. Two downsides to this approach are that the data can be more difficult to analyze, and the non-anonymous nature of some interviews (i.e., the interviewer knows who is saying what) could influence more guarded responses on sensitive issues. If this approach is used, we recommend that the interviewer use a standard set of questions across all participants to ensure comparability of responses, and that steps to ensure confidentiality be created and communicated.

Another method for data collection is the *focus group*, essentially an interview conducted with a larger group (e.g., 2–8 participants). This approach too can result in rich information due to the ability to ask follow-up probes, but also because participants sometimes build upon and add to others' responses to an evaluation question, or prompt additional thoughts from another participant, building a more synergistic response. Again, the data can be difficult to analyze, and because anonymity is reduced further due to multiple participants being present, some sensitive information may not be communicated. For this reason, in addition to using a standardized question protocol as with interviews, we recommend that program evaluators offer focus group participants the opportunity to have one-on-one interviews if they are concerned about sharing sensitive information.

Surveys and questionnaires are often used to measure the success of organizational development initiatives, and are quite applicable to formal mentoring programs. These instruments can be used to gather both qualitative (e.g., open-ended comments about a program's strengths) and quantitative information (e.g., ratings of the program's value). Learning is often measured via questionnaires of some sort. Although results are typically measured at the individual level, when combined across all participants in a mentoring program, results can approximate organizational level variables as well. For example, typically a survey will measure a specific person's job satisfaction, yet when each participant's job satisfaction results are averaged together across all participants, what results is an overall job satisfaction score that reflects more on the overall climate of the group. The benefits to questionnaires are that they are relatively inexpensive, easy to administer, allow for quick and relatively easy numerical calculations and comparisons, and permit the evaluator to gather a large amount of data. However, the richness of questionnaire data is sometimes limited due to the inability to immediately follow-up and probe on participants' responses, and sometimes the wording of items can be confusing or misleading.

Other *organizational measures* that are not designed specifically for the mentoring program can also be used to measure results nonetheless. These may include 360-degree feedback surveys that measure the protégé's behavior or performance change, performance appraisal reviews that measure the protégé's behavior or performance change, company financial results that measure cost and revenue information, and HR data systems that measure turnover and retention statistics.

There is not one blanket recommendation that can be made in terms of what tool or tools to use to measure results. For a small mentoring program with 10 or fewer participants, one-on-one interviews may be the most economical and rich approach, whereas for a much larger number of participants a survey may be a good first step, followed by focus groups and interviews to probe the results more in-depth. The goals of the program will also direct practitioners as to what tools to use.

Data Tracking System

Regardless of what tools are used to measure results, programs should establish a system for managing program information in an efficient way. Such a system should include a mechanism for analyzing data over time. Data to be tracked includes program finances. Records should also be kept regarding all mentors and protégés, the dates that relationships contractually began and ended, demographic information on mentors and protégés, and who was matched with whom. This information can be particularly useful for fine-tuning the matching process. Keeping detailed program records plays a key part in the monitoring and evaluation process. The data can be used to inform stakeholders, partner organizations or the project team.

Whom to Measure

The next consideration for organizations is to determine who will provide input into the evaluation measures. Although this may seem logical at first, some thought should be given as to who is the person(s) in the best position to provide valid information on each of the measures. Clearly, both mentors and protégés will be a primary source of information. Protégés can be assessed as to what they have learned from their mentoring experience, how they have improved their performance, what skills have they gained, etc. They can also provide evidence as to how well their mentors performed, as well as what improvements need to be made to the mentoring program. Likewise, mentors can provide a second-person assessment of the protégé's learning, growth, and performance improvement, in addition to program improvement opportunities. We also believe it important to assess how and in what ways mentors benefited from the mentoring experience, as research indicates their commitment to the program is related to how much they benefit.

Other organizational stakeholders can provide input as well. A protégé's supervisor, for example, is a prime source of information for assessing the protégé's performance and behavior change. If the protégé has direct reports, they can be used as information resources as well. This type of input is often gathered via 360-degree feedback surveys. If the protégé's development plan required him or her to interact or work with peers, executives, or customers, they can be sought for information as well. This may be particularly advantageous if the purpose of the mentoring program is to prepare the protégé for expanded, higher-level responsibilities that require him or her to interact with a broader set of colleagues. For example, if a protégé is being prepared for executive-level responsibilities, and is given the opportunity to make a presentation before a group of executives, then those executives may be the most important source of feedback to measure the protégé's executive presence, communication ability, and presentation skills.

Case Study:
Monitoring and Evaluation

This case study references a leading global energy company engaged in exploring and producing crude oil and natural gas, and in refining and marketing petroleum products, natural gas, and electricity. The goal of the company's mentoring program is to support its talent and succession planning process by offering developmental opportunities for high-potential employees as well as helping the on-boarding of employees in high impact jobs.

According to the Director of Talent Management and Organizational Development, one of the key features of the company's program is its thorough monitoring and evaluation process. "Check-ins" are conducted for each mentoring relationship on a quarterly basis, whereby the program's administrator will meet separately with the mentor and protégé to assess how well the relationship is working, what is not working well, and what needs to be changed. Also, three to four times a year, mentors are asked to speak about their challenges and experiences, and to seek assistance, from the executive mentoring committee that oversees the program. At the one-year time frame (the recommended length for a typical mentoring relationship), quantitative and qualitative surveys are distributed to both mentors and protégés to evaluate the success of the program (e.g., were their expectations met; what can be done to improve the program).

The mentoring committee reviews results from the monitoring and evaluation processes in order to highlight potential problems and issues, make immediate corrections (e.g., changing mentor–protégé pairings), and/or suggest permanent changes and improvements to the program. The advantage to using a committee approach is that a wider range of perspectives is brought forth to enhance the program's effectiveness. Partially as a result of the aforementioned monitoring and evaluation steps, mentoring relationships that were not working well were improved, and the program has been targeted for expansion to a wider range of employees.

Timing of the Evaluation

Another issue to consider is the timing of the evaluation. To a large degree, *when* to measure results will depend on *what* is being measured and *how* it is being measured. For example, many organizational change experts argue that it takes at least six months to one year for change to occur. Likewise, it can take several months before an individual has had enough training, experience, and practice in order to fully learn and apply a new skill. For this reason, many mentoring programs structure their relationships for a minimum of six months. Therefore, outcome measures that are more performance-, behavior-, or results-oriented (i.e., Kirkpatrick's levels 3 and 4) are most appropriately measured at the end of the contracted mentoring period. This does not preclude an organization from making mid-term assessments to measure progress and see if results are on track with intended goals. Regardless, in order to allow time for true change to occur, we recommend that the final assessment of behavior, performance, and results occur at a minimum of when the contracted relationship ends, preferably six months or longer.

On the other hand, other results may be measured more often and closer to the event or situation. For example, it may be possible to gauge participants' reactions to different steps or mentoring processes as soon as they have occurred via a short survey or a quick interview, e.g., after training; after the first mentor–protégé meeting; after the mid-term monitoring session; after the relationship has ended. These results can be combined to look at patterns and trends over time (e.g., do participants' satisfaction levels increase over time as the relationship becomes more grounded?), as well as spot emerging problem areas that can quickly be corrected. Learning is another type of measure that may be evaluated at several points of the mentoring program. For example, a test could be administered before and after the training program to determine how much the participants have learned during the training program. This would help program administrators follow up with participants to ensure they have the information they need, and when combined with reaction data, could possibly suggest changes to the training program. Waiting until the mentoring relationship has ended, 6–12 months later, to measure these results could result in missed opportunities and information.

Therefore, it is our recommendation that organizations not look to just measure success at one point in time. Rather, based on the program's goals, structure of the program, and resources available, organizations should measure results at multiple points in time, tailored to the type of result being measured.

Evaluation Design

In order to conduct a scientifically sound evaluation, an organization should gather results from a comparison or control group of employees who did not have access to mentoring, as well as pre- and post-mentoring comparisons to determine the amount of attitudinal, behavioral, or performance change experienced. This pretest-posttest control group design is not without its problems, yet it can provide valid information about a program's effectiveness and help rule out the influence of non-mentoring related factors on results. Without such a design it is difficult to reliably attribute success to the program (i.e., a protégé's performance improvement could have resulted from something other than the mentoring program).

Ideally, a true experimental design using randomization is recommended. In this design, a company would screen and select its group of protégés as usual (e.g., newly hired employees; new managers; high potential employees). Then, half of the participants would be randomly assigned to a control group, and the other half would be randomly assigned to the mentoring group. The mentoring group would receive mentoring as designed, whereas the control group would not. By randomly assigning participants into these groups, several competing explanations and biases to the results can be controlled, thus leading to much more valid conclusions about the effectiveness of the program.

However, in many organizations a true experimental study is not feasible (e.g., fairness and resource utilization concerns resulting from denying one group of participants the opportunity to develop). One strategy to combat this problem is to create a list of potential protégés and then randomly divide them in half, with one half participating in the mentoring program immediately, and the other half placed on a waiting list but used as a control group in the first round of mentoring (i.e., they will not receive mentoring initially but will at a later date). A hidden benefit to this approach is that the results from the evaluation of the first round of mentoring can be used to make valid improvements to the program. Thus, when the control group does participate as protégés in the second round of mentoring, they will be going through a stronger program.

The recommendation to provide a control group creates an evaluation plan that will permit the most confidence in attributing positive changes to the impact of the mentoring program. However, conducting an evaluation without a control group can still provide valuable information and is certainly better than conducting no evaluation.

What we have described thus far might be referred to as a goals-based evaluation. That is, the evaluation is conducted with the primary focus of determining if the objective(s) of the program have been met. However, evaluations can also be conducted to compare variations in elements of the program. It can be important not only to examine the impact of the program as a whole but also to investigate how alterations in the program may affect outcomes. Thus, another way of conducting an evaluation is to vary aspects of the program itself. For example, the way in which participants are matched and/or trained could be varied across multiple groups and then compared across the outcomes of interest. Specifically, one group of protégés (ideally randomly assigned) could be matched with mentors based on specific factors (e.g., functional areas, interests, personality), whereas another group could be matched with mentors in a random manner. Evaluations of the relationship, learning, performance improvement, etc., can be made comparing the systematically and randomly assigned groups to see if one matching process results in more favorable outcomes. This level of experimental design requires careful planning and execution, yet the results can be infinitely more robust than those gathered from a single survey administered at the end of the mentoring relationship with no control or comparison groups.

Action Plan:
Monitoring and Evaluation

- Plan how often you will check in with the mentors and protégés throughout the mentorships.
- Decide whether these check-ins will involve surveys, individual meetings, or group meetings (or a mix of these methods).
- Create a list of questions to be used for the check-ins.
- Determine a step-by-step plan for handling problems within matches. Ideally this is something that the pairs will be informed of during orientation.
- Decide how the data gathered will be tracked and analyzed, who will be responsible for that, and who will see the data.
- Based on the program objectives (Chapter 1), select or create the appropriate program evaluation criteria.
- Determine whether measures will be qualitative, quantitative, or both.
- Decide what measures should focus on the individual level and what should focus on the organizational level.
- Determine what reactions you would like to garner from participants and create appropriate reaction measures.
- If learning was a measurable objective determined at the outset, create or select a measure to assess the level of learning. Ideally there will be a pre- and post-measure to look for change.
- If specific behavior/performance change was a measurable objective determined at the outset, create or select a measure to assess that behavioral change. Ideally there will be a pre-and post-measure to look for change.

- If organizational-level business results were a measurable objective determined at the outset, decide which business metrics will be examined and how the impact of other business factors on those metrics will be controlled.
- Decide the method for collecting these evaluations (e.g., individual meetings, focus groups, surveys). Ideally if methodological control is feasible, assignment of participants to groups should be considered earlier on in the process.
- Determine whether other organizational stakeholders besides participants in the program should provide input for the measures and gain their cooperation in the process.
- Create a timeline for when various measures will be taken, and task individuals on the mentoring committee with carrying out the process.

Afterword

We hope you finish this book with an appreciation of the potential of a well-designed and executed formal organizational mentoring program. Depending on the program's goals, mentoring could enhance recruitment and retention, increase learning and satisfaction, build a diverse talent base, and revitalize careers. Although a mentoring program is not a stand-alone panacea, as a key component of an organization's talent management strategy it can have dynamic and powerful results for protégés, mentors, and the organization.

Using the scientific research base on mentoring as our guide, we have provided a step-by-step guide for practitioners who wish to build a formal mentoring program. The chapters in this book move from the starting line – planning and developing the necessary infrastructure – through the many decisions to be made and action steps to be taken along the way, including choosing participants, matching, training, structuring processes, monitoring progress, and evaluating outcomes.

Although it has been stressed throughout this volume, it bears repeating one last time: there is no one best way to structure and implement a mentoring program that will work equally well in all organizations. That means that there is no strict recipe to follow that is guaranteed to produce a successful outcome every time. Fortunately, there are clear steps to follow to aid in making the best decisions for your own situation. Throughout the book we have provided several tools to assist in the process, and we encourage you to customize and use them however you consider best. We also cannot stress enough the benefit that sound evaluation research could have, not only to your program, but, if shared with the scientist-practitioner community, to the field as a whole.

If as you put down this book, you are now considering taking on a mentoring program, we wish you the best of luck in your challenging, exciting, and rewarding endeavor.

Appendix A: Formal Mentoring Program

Scope and Planning Form

Step 1: Laying the Foundation

Overall Purpose. What is the essential question or problem that is to be addressed by the formal mentoring program? Why is it being created?

Mission Statement. What is the underlying philosophy or vision that will guide the design and implementation of the formal mentoring program?

Goals. What are the specific goals and outcomes to be accomplished by the formal mentoring program? Be sure to make these goals as specific, measurable, and achievable as possible.

Alignment with Strategy. How will the formal mentoring program contribute to the company's overall business strategy?

Continued

Alignment with Culture. In what ways will the formal mentoring program be consistent with the company's overall culture?

Integration. What existing programs within the organization can be linked with and support the mentoring program to create synergy? How will formal mentoring be integrated with these programs?

Step 2: Framing the Structure

Organizational Support. Who is the driver or sponsor of the program? In what specific ways will he, she, or they demonstrate their support for the program?

Communication. How will information about the program be communicated? To what populations will the mentoring program be communicated? What methods will be used?

Unit Participants. Which organizational units will participate in the mentoring program?

Target Population. What population is the mentoring program designed to target? Will the program target a specific gender and or ethnic group for participation?

Skills and Issues. What skills or issues will the mentoring program address?

- ❑ Diversity Initiative
- ❑ Leadership Development
- ❑ New Employee Socialization
- ❑ Knowledge Development
- ❑ Talent Retention
- ❑ Succession Planning
- ❑ Work/Family Support
- ❑ Job Training
- ❑ Network Building

Resource Requirements. What resources are needed to successfully implement, operate, and maintain the program?

People: _____

Time: _____

Financial: _____

Administration. Which unit will manage the program? Who will be the program administrator?

Step 3: Installing the Walls

Number of Participants. How many people are targeted to participate as protégés? As mentors?

Recruiting Mentors. How will mentors be identified and recruited? What characteristics are desired and/or required of mentors?

❑ Levels above Protégé   ❑ Willingness to Mentor

❑ Years of Leadership Experience   ❑ Knowledge and Skills to be a Mentor

❑ Availability of Time   ❑ Previous Mentoring Experience

Recruiting Protégés. How will protégés be identified and recruited? What characteristics are desired and/or required of protégés?

❑ Levels below Mentor   ❑ Openness to Experience and Learning

❑ Organizational Tenure   ❑ High-Potential for Targeted Promotion

❑ Part of Target Population   ❑ Recent Promotion

Participant Requirements. Will participation in the program be mandatory or voluntary for protégés? For mentors? Why? How will objections be overcome? How will exceptions be handled?

Time Commitment. What will be the time commitment for the mentoring relationship?

What will be the number of meetings/hours per month?

_____

What will be the length of the mentoring relationship (e.g., 6 months, 1 year)?

_____

Matching. How will mentors and protégés be matched? Who will do the matching? What characteristics will be considered (e.g., physical distance, developmental gaps)?

Training. Will the program include training for protégés? For mentors? Which topics will be included? Who will conduct the training?

☐ Overview/Goals of Program   ☐ Creating Trust
☐ Roles and Responsibilities   ☐ Participation Requirements
☐ Obstacles to Avoid   ☐ Giving and Receiving Feedback
☐ Conflict Management Skills   ☐ How to Network
☐ Developmental Action Planning

Step 4: Maintaining the Program

Obstacles and Challenges. What challenges or obstacles do you anticipate in implementing and maintaining the program? How will these be overcome?

Protégé Support. How will the program provide on-going support for protégés?

Mentor Support. How will the program provide on-going support for mentors?

Monitoring. What methods or steps will be taken to monitor the progress of mentoring relationships? How often will check-ins be conducted? Who will initiate the check-in?

Method	Frequency	Responsibility
❑ Phone Call	❑ Monthly	❑ Program Administrator
❑ Email Updates	❑ Bi-monthly	❑ Protégé
❑ Personal Interview	❑ Quarterly	❑ Mentor
❑ Formal Survey	❑ Semi-annually	❑ Other (Specify: _____)

Evaluation. How will the success of the program be evaluated?

❑ Interviews   ❑ Focus Groups
❑ Reaction Surveys   ❑ Evaluation of Statistics
❑ Other (Specify:_____)

Appendix B: Formal Mentoring Program Needs Assessment

Possible Interview/Focus Group Questions

Organizational Assessment

1. What are the strengths of the company's current systems and processes for employee development and socialization?
2. What are the weaknesses of the company's current systems and processes for employee development and socialization? What gaps exist?
3. How will a formal mentoring program address any gaps in the organization's current developmental processes? How will it integrate with other existing systems?
4. What business objectives and goals will be addressed by a formal mentoring program?
5. What resources are to be committed to the formal mentoring program?
6. Who is going to be the champion of the program? How will he/she/they champion the program?
7. Who will "own" and administer the program?
8. What units/divisions/functions of the company will participate?
9. Based on past experience, what obstacles will this program encounter? How can they be overcome?

Design Assessment

1. If an ideal system were to be built, what do you believe would be the key features and characteristics of the mentoring program?
2. Should protégé and/or mentor participation be mandatory? Why or why not?
3. What issues, goals, needs, etc., should the mentoring program focus on addressing (e.g., employee skill development; socialization; increasing networks; broadening exposure; retaining employees; giving minority and female employees more visibility)?
4. How long should the mentoring relationship last?
5. How often should mentors and protégés be required to meet? How should they meet (e.g., face-to-face; phone)?
6. How should the mentoring relationship be monitored? External party? By the pair? How often should they be monitored?
7. How should the program be evaluated?
8. What should happen if a mentoring relationship encounters problems?

Resource Assessment

1. Who should be allowed to participate as mentors? As protégés?
2. Should mentors and protégés be matched together by some external process, or should they pair up on their own? Why do you say this?
3. What characteristics should be considered in matching protégés and mentors?
4. Should mentors and/or protégés be rewarded for their participation? If so, how?
5. What role should mentors and protégés have in determining how their relationship will carry out, what activities they will undertake, how long their relationship will last, and what goals and issues they will address?

Appendix C: Mentor Readiness Assessment

Part I: Ability

Review the statements listed below and think about your own readiness to be a mentor. In the blank space beside each statement, write down the number that corresponds to your readiness to perform that particular mentor behavior. Use the following scale when making your response.

1 = Not ready at all   **2** = Somewhat Ready   **3** = Definitely Ready

_____ 1. Help the protégé make contacts with senior leaders in the organization.

_____ 2. Provide positive recognition and constructive feedback to the protégé.

_____ 3. Share your knowledge of the organization's unwritten rules.

_____ 4. Give the protégé assignments that expose him or her to key figures in the organization.

_____ 5. Role model the way things get done.

_____ 6. Help the protégé develop a career path.

_____ 7. Give the protégé developmental guidance and advice, as needed.

_____ 8. Keep the protégé appraised of important events and goings-on.

_____ 9. Help the protégé diagnose and assess his or her developmental needs.

_____ 10. Provide the protégé with challenging assignments.

Part II: Commitment and Willingness

Review the statements listed below and check the answer that is most appropriate for you.

	Yes	No
1. Are you willing to invest time, energy, and effort in a mentoring relationship?	❏	❏
2. Are you willing to help the protégé learn from his or her challenges and mistakes?	❏	❏
3. Are you willing to give honest feedback to the protégé'?	❏	❏
4. Are you willing to share the learning from your failures as well as your successes?	❏	❏

5. Listed below are some common concerns as well as potential benefits. Check those concerns and benefits most important to you.

Concerns	Benefits
❏ Time Commitment	❏ Opportunity to Help Someone Develop
❏ Perceptions of Bias and Fairness	❏ Opportunity to Improve My Coaching and Feedback Skills
❏ Lack of Chemistry with Protégé	❏ Contribute to the Company's Success
❏ Any Problems Will Be Held Against Me	❏ Leave a Legacy with the Company
❏ My Ability to Provide Valuable Experiences	❏ Build My Support Network
❏ My Ability to Coach and Give Feedback	

6. Do the benefits outweigh the concerns?   ❏   ❏

Appendix D: Protégé Screening Form

Review the employee's performance and check the box to indicate which knowledge, skill, ability, or other characteristic the employee currently has that would make him or her a candidate for mentoring. Provide evidence and examples to justify your ratings.

KNOWLEDGE, SKILLS, ABILITIES	
❑ Listening Skills ❑ Communication Skills ❑ Interpersonal Sensitivity ❑ Ability to Build Relationships ❑ Leadership Ability	Comments and Observations
PERSONALITY CHARACTERISTICS	
❑ Willingness to Learn ❑ Openness to Constructive Feedback ❑ Strong Work Ethic ❑ Achievement Orientation ❑ Extraversion	Comments and Observations
INDIVIDUAL CHARACTERISTICS & ATTITUDES	
❑ Initiative ❑ Commitment to Organization ❑ Job Involvement ❑ Job Satisfaction	Comments and Observations

Please answer the following questions completely in order that a fair and objective decision can be made regarding this employee's potential as a protégé in the formal mentoring program.

Why should this employee be a protégé/receive mentoring?

How will having this employee be a protégé benefit our company?

What are the top three outcomes you expect the employee to achieve as a result of being a protégé in the formal mentoring program?

What obstacles or concerns do you have about the employee's readiness and willingness to be an effective protégé?

Appendix E: Mentor Profile Form

Part 1: Please complete all sections of this form in order that the mentoring committee can learn as much about your background as possible. This information will be used only to pair you with a suitable protégé.

Current job role and responsibilities

How long have you worked in this job? How long have you worked in the company?

Knowledge, skills, and abilities required to perform your job (Check those that apply)

- ❏ Influence
- ❏ Planning & Organization
- ❏ Adaptability
- ❏ Oral Communication
- ❏ Written Communication
- ❏ Stress Tolerance
- ❏ Interpersonal Skills
- ❏ Change Management
- ❏ Others (_____)
- ❏ Technical Knowledge: (List areas below)
- •
- •

- ❏ Strategic Thinking
- ❏ Leadership/Motivation
- ❏ Coach & Develop Others
- ❏ Problem Solving
- ❏ Customer Focus
- ❏ Teamwork
- ❏ Decision Making
- ❏ Delegation

- •
- •

What knowledge, skills, or abilities do you believe you excel at? (List from above)

Continued

Educational background (degree(s), school(s), when graduated)

Divisions/departments/functions other than yours that you interact/work with

Hobbies and interests

Part 2: Please answer the following questions as completely as possible. This information will be used only to pair you with a suitable protégé.

What do you hope to gain by being a mentor?
What are you looking for in your ideal protégé? What abilities, skills, personality characteristics, and knowledge areas would he or she have?
What are you hoping you can provide to your protégé? In what ways or areas can you help him or her the most?
How often do you travel as part of your job?
What do you foresee as the major obstacles you will encounter in providing quality mentoring (e.g., time, availability, travel schedule, location, work schedule)?

Appendix F: Protégé Profile Form

Part 1: Please complete all sections of this form in order that the mentoring committee can learn as much about your background as possible. This information will be used only to pair you with a suitable mentor.

Current job role and responsibilities
How long have you worked in this job? How long have you worked in the company?
What are your 3-year career goals? 5 years? 10 years?
What knowledge, skills, or abilities do you believe you excel at?

What knowledge, skills, or abilities do you believe you need further development in to reach your career goals?

Educational background (degree(s), school(s), when graduated)

Hobbies and interests

Part 2: Please answer the following questions as completely as possible. This information will be used only to pair you with a suitable mentor.

What do you hope to gain by having a mentor?

What activities are you expecting your mentor to undertake in your development?

What skills, abilities, personality characteristics, and knowledge areas do you want your mentor to have?

In what ways can you help or provide value to your mentor?

How often do you travel as part of your job?

What do you foresee as the major obstacles you will encounter in participating in the mentoring relationship (e.g., time, availability, travel schedule, location, work schedule)?

Appendix G: Sample Training Outline

Title of Program	Being an Effective Mentor or Protégé
Description of Program	This course is designed to provide managers and employees with the knowledge, skills, and abilities that they will need in order to participate effectively as mentors and/or protégés in Acme's "Developing the Leaders of Tomorrow Today" formal mentoring program.
Training Objectives	After attending this course, mentors and protégés will be able to: • Define what mentoring is and how it is different from other developmental activities (e.g., coaching) • Understand how Acme's formal mentoring program operates • Understand the intended outcomes, benefits, and drawbacks of participation in the formal mentoring program • Demonstrate the skills, behaviors, and characteristics needed to be an effective mentor or protégé • Understand the roles in facilitating an effective mentoring relationship • Create clear expectations, goals, and development plans • Resolve conflicts and problems that might arise
Intended Audience	Managers and employees who have been selected to participate as either mentors or protégés in Acme's "Developing the Leaders of Tomorrow Today" formal mentoring program.
Location & Time	Corporate Building, Room H231, 8:00AM, Thursday, September 27

Appendix H: Sample Training Schedule

Course: Formal Mentoring Training for "Developing the Leaders of Tomorrow Today"

Time	Topics	Delivery Methods
7:30am–8:00am	*Sign in and Continental Breakfast*	N/A
8:00am–8:45am	*Welcome and Overview* • Participant introductions • Review course objectives • Review course schedules • Gather participant goals and expectations • Review ground-rules for the course	• Lecture • Participant introductions • Warm-up activity
8:45am–10:30am	*What is Mentoring?* • Definition and types of mentoring • Benefits and risks of mentoring • What a mentor does • What a protégé does • Types of mentoring relationships	• Lecture • Participant discussion • Review participants' examples of effective and non-effective mentoring • Video testimonials
10:30am–10:45am	BREAK	
10:45am–12:00pm	*Acme's "Developing the Leaders of Tomorrow Today" Formal Mentoring Program* • History of program • Program timeline • Outcomes and limitations of program • How the program operates (e.g., matching process; evaluation and monitoring) • Using the web-based "Experience and Skill Database System"	• Lecture • Participant discussion • Demonstration • Practice using tools

12:00pm–12:45pm	LUNCH	
12:45pm–4:00pm	**SEPARATE PROTÉGÉ AND MENTOR TRAINING**	See next page
4:00pm–4:45pm	*Making the Most of Mentoring* • Overcoming common obstacles and problems • Tips for making the most of the mentoring relationship	• Lecture • Participant discussion
4:45pm–5:30pm	*Negotiating a Mentoring Agreement* • Mentoring Agreement Document	• Lecture • Activity: Using ACME's formal mentoring agreement form, mentoring dyads will begin to structure a formal mentoring agreement
5:30pm–6:00pm	*Course Wrap-up* • Learning and Course Evaluation	• Wrap-up activity
6:00pm–7:00pm	*Dinner and Social Hour*	• Encourage discussion among mentoring pairs

After lunch, separate training participants into two groups: mentors and protégés. From 12:45pm–4:00pm each group will receive separate training with a separate facilitator. Mentors will stay in the current room, whereas protégés will move to another room.

At 4:00pm, protégés and mentors will reconvene in the main training room for the remainder of the training course.

Mentor Training

Time	Topics	Delivery Methods
12:45pm–1:30pm	*Roles and Responsibilities of a Mentor* • Key activities of a mentor • Different mentoring techniques • What protégés want from their mentors	• Lecture • Participant discussion
1:30pm–4:00pm	*Mentor KSAs* • Key knowledge, skills and abilities needed to be an effective mentor • Creating a development plan • Delivering feedback • Handling conflict	• Lecture • Participant discussion • Activity 1: Case study in creating a development plan • Activity 2: Role-play in giving feedback • Activity 3: Role-play in resolving conflict • Video demonstration

Protégé Training

Time	Topics	Delivery Methods
12:45pm–1:30pm	*Roles and Responsibilities of a Protégé* • Key activities of a protégé • Different mentoring techniques • What mentors want from their protégés	• Lecture • Participant discussion
1:30pm–4:00pm	*Protégé KSAs* • Key knowledge, skills and abilities needed to be an effective protégé • Understand your learning style • Receiving constructive feedback • Handling conflict	• Lecture • Participant discussion • Activity 1: Complete and discuss learning style inventory • Activity 2: Role-play in receiving feedback • Activity 3: Role-play in resolving conflict • Video demonstration

Appendix I: Sample Training Activity

Activity: Receiving Constructive Feedback

Purpose
This activity gives participants practice at receiving feedback and working through mentoring-related performance issues with their mentor. Listening, communication, and openness to learning are the skills that are reinforced.

Vignette
The mentor has observed the protégé make a formal presentation to senior executives, and has scheduled a feedback session to provide positive and negative feedback. The mentor role calls for the role-player to do three things that require the protégé role-player to use listening, communication, and questioning skills: (1) start providing negative feedback before positive feedback; (2) deliver vague and non-specific feedback (e.g., "You weren't communicating well enough"), and (3) not offer any advice, guidance, or solutions to help the protégé improve. If the protégé role-player uses effective listening and questioning, then the mentor role-player will become more specific and helpful with feedback and guidance.

Instructions
1. Divide the class into two groups. Half will role-play the mentor, the other half will role-play the protégé. Pair people up into mentor–protégé dyads.
2. Hand out the background documents to participants: mentor documents go to the participants role-playing the mentor, and protégé documents go to the participants role-playing the protégé.
3. Give participants 15 minutes to familiarize themselves with the background materials. Then, instruct them to play out their roles for 10 minutes. Strongly encourage the protégés to practice the listening, communication, and questioning skills they learned during the instruction module.
4. As participants are role-playing, walk the room and listen into each of the role-plays, noting the effective and ineffective behaviors being demonstrated.
5. After 15 minutes, stop the exercise. Lead a 10-minute discussion on what participants found helpful in receiving and working with the feedback, as well as what did not work. Ask participants what they learned most. Share your observations of effective and ineffective techniques.

6. Ask participants to switch roles and background information, and repeat steps 3 through 5.

Total Time Required
1 hour and 15 minutes

Activity: Resolving Difficult Situations

Purpose
This activity gives participants practice at working with their protégé through a typical mentoring conflict. Listening, communication, and conflict resolution are the skills that are reinforced.

Vignette
The protégé has requested an "emergency" meeting with the mentor to discuss some problems he or she is having with the relationship. Some of these problems are alluded to in the email the protégé sent the mentor (which the mentor will review), but during the meeting the problems will be expanded upon and new issues will be brought up. The mentor will have to use listening, emotional control, communication, and questioning skills to defuse the situation, convey support, and build an action plan moving forward.

Instructions
1. Divide the class into two groups. Half will role-play the mentor, the other half will role-play the protégé. Pair people up into mentor–protégé dyads.
2. Hand out the background documents to participants: mentor documents go to the participants role-playing the mentor, and protégé documents go to the participants role-playing the protégé.
3. Give participants 20 minutes to familiarize themselves with the background materials. Then, instruct them to play out their roles for 15 minutes. Strongly encourage the mentors to practice the listening, communication, and questioning skills they learned during the instruction module.
4. As participants are role-playing, walk the room and listen into each of the role-plays, noting the effective and ineffective behaviors being demonstrated.
5. After 15 minutes, stop the exercise. Lead a 10-minute discussion on what participants found helpful in working through the problem, as well as what did not work. Ask participants what they learned most. Share your observations of effective and ineffective techniques.

6. Ask participants to switch roles and background information, and repeat steps 3 through 5.

Total Time Required
1 hour and 30 minutes

Resolving Difficult Situations

Mentor Role-Play Instructions

The purpose of this exercise is to give you practice at working through difficult situations that you may encounter when mentoring your protégé. You should rely on the instruction you received and the skills you learned during the last training module in order to complete this exercise successfully.

For this exercise, you are the Senior Vice President of ACME, Inc., an engineering and architecture firm. Today is September 27, 2008. You are two months into a mentoring relationship with Robin Public, a Senior Engineer in the Design Division who has 6 years' tenure with the company. As part of Robin's leadership development, you and Robin agreed to give Robin more industry and organizational knowledge, broaden Robin's network of contacts, and work to improve Robin's public speaking skills. Some progress has been made, but as it is early in the relationship much more is left to be done. A progress report that was completed by the program administrator for your relationship is included in this packet of materials.

Two days, Robin requested a meeting with you to discuss some concerns he/she is having with the mentoring relationship. Robin is expecting that by the end of the meeting to have an action plan in place to deal with these concerns. It will be your job to uncover what these issues are, what is causing them, and what can be done to address them. As your company has invested significant resources into making formal mentoring a key business strategy, your program administrator is expecting that you will make every effort to save the relationship.

Your instructions are to review the attached materials for 20 minutes, then Robin will enter your office to begin the meeting. You should plan on meeting with Robin for 15 minutes. After the exercise the entire class will reconvene.

Remember to utilize the skills and information you learned during the training session.

Email

To: Mentor, Senior Vice President

From: Robin Public

Re: Emergency Meeting

Sorry to have to email you, but my cell phone is on the brink right now and I am on the road. I wonder if you would be able to meet with me in the next couple of days to discuss some issues and concerns I am having with our mentoring relationship. I want this to work out, so I hope to be able to air my concerns in an open and collaborative setting. Basically, I don't think I have been getting enough opportunity to develop, and I want some things to change.

Please let me know if and when we can meet.

ACME, Inc.
PERSONNEL FORM

Employee Name: Robin Public

Employment Date: June 15, 2002

Job Titles: Engineer I: 6/15/02–3/28/05
               Engineer II: 3/29/05–1/15/08
               Senior Engineer: 1/16/08–current

Overall Job Performance Rating (Unacceptable, Marginal, Acceptable, Commendable, Outstanding):
               2002: Acceptable
               2003: Commendable
               2004: Outstanding
               2005 (through 3/28/05): Outstanding
               2005 (3/29/05–12/31/05): Commendable
               2006: Outstanding
               2007: Outstanding
               2008 (through 1/15/08): Outstanding

Current Status: – Senior Engineer
               – Identified as High Potential, Selected as Protégé in "Developing the Leaders of Tomorrow Today" Formal Mentoring Program

Career Goals: Senior Executive position in Engineering

"Leaders of Tomorrow"
Formal Mentoring Program
Progress Report

Date Printed: September 27, 2008
Completed by: You

Objective 1: Develop Robin's industry and organizational knowledge

Actions Taken: (1) Provided Robin with several marketing reports, background materials, annual reports, executive letters, and historical information in order to learn more about the background and growth of ACME; (2) provided Robin with marketing and competitor analysis reports for our top five competitors.

Actions Planned: (1) Intend to discuss these materials with Robin at a date/meeting not yet scheduled; (2) have Robin accompany me to the next Annual Meeting for American Engineering Association to learn about the organization and meet new contacts; and, (3) require Robin to research, identify, and analyze the top five issues impacting our industry for the next 10 years.

Success to Date: Robin has indicated to me that he/she has not had time to read the materials given, as he/she is still adapting to the increased demands of the Senior Engineer position.

Comments: Robin does not seem to have much motivation to work in this area. When I have asked what else Robin would like to do, I do not get any answers. I need to research ways to give Robin this information other than reading, perhaps by scheduling short meetings with retired executives and managers to discuss more about the company's background, as well as meetings with VPs from other divisions/functions in order to learn more about what they do. Need to run this by Robin.

Objective 2: Broaden Robin's network

Actions Taken: (1) Took Robin to the most recent Monthly Executive Management Status Report meeting – introduced Robin to three of my peer executives; (2) Requested Robin to complete the "Network Spider Web" activity in order to determine the strength and scope of

Robin's current network; (3) counseled Robin, who is a naturally quiet and introverted individual, on how to build quick rapport with others.

Actions Planned: (1) Have Robin accompany me to the next Annual Meeting for American Engineering Association to learn about the organization and meet new contacts; (2) continue to take Robin to Monthly Executive Management Status Report meetings and introduce Robin to three new people each meeting; (3) map out with Robin what other contacts are needed and what benefits those would bring; and, (4) continue to help Robin develop relationship building skills.

Success to Date: Robin has maintained regular contact with one contact from the executive meeting; in my estimation, Robin seemed uncomfortable and lacking confidence when talking to these executives ... would often remain quiet. Spider Web activity is not completed.

Comments: I need to do more one-on-one counseling and coaching with Robin on how to build rapport in order that Robin can have greater confidence when meeting others. Need to hold Robin accountable for completing the exercise and explain its importance in learning where to target our networking efforts.

Objective 3: Improve Robin's public speaking skills

Actions Taken: Scheduled Robin for a Public Speaking training course offered by the company – not yet taken place due to scheduling difficulties.

Actions Planned: (1) Take the public speaking course; (2) Robin will make the status report presentation for my division at the next Monthly Executive Management Status Report meeting; (3) Robin will run our exhibitor's booth at the next Annual Meeting for American Engineering Association and speak with potential clients about our products and services; (4) have Robin accompany me to other formal meetings and presentations to observe other accomplished speakers; and, (5) provide continual feedback to Robin in this area.

Success to Date: N/A

Comments: I do not believe I have been doing as much as I could to help Robin in this area. I do not have any meetings scheduled with other speakers, and until Robin takes the public speaking course and practices, I would not feel comfortable having Robin speak for my division. I need to do more here.

OVERALL COMMENTS

My division was recently expanding two-fold as another division was merged into mine. Handling the various administrative, scheduling, structure, and organizational issues has taken up a great deal of my time. Therefore, I likely have not given the attention to this relationship that I should.

At the same time, I find that Robin is extremely dependent upon me to get things done. I have had to schedule our first four meetings. I have to request status updates from Robin rather than them being provided to me. I have to come up with the developmental ideas and actions, as Robin has not offered any solutions. I fear Robin may become too dependent upon me if this continues.

Resolving Difficult Situations

Protégé Role-Play Instructions

In this exercise, you will be playing the role of Robin Public, a Senior Engineer at ACME, Inc., an engineering and architecture firm. You are two months into a formal mentoring relationship with a Senior Vice President. You are in the formal mentoring program because you have been identified as a high potential employee. As part of your leadership development, you and your mentor agreed to increase your industry and organizational knowledge, broaden your network of contacts, and work to improve your public speaking skills.

From your perspective, the mentoring relationship has not been meeting your expectations. Therefore, you sent an email to your mentor requesting a meeting to discuss your concerns and create a plan to address them. A copy of this email is attached to these documents.

A copy of your personnel history is also attached. You have been working at the company for just over 6 years. Your annual performance ratings have always been Commendable to Outstanding. However, since your promotion to Senior Engineer this past January, you have been struggling with the additional responsibilities of managing projects and managing project teams. At your current level of performance, you will be lucky to get a rating of Acceptable (the midpoint of the rating scale, indicating average performance).

Trying to be a good participant in the mentoring program while managing your job duties has been stressful. You do not feel you have put as much effort into the program as you could . . . you really don't have many ideas as to how to achieve your mentoring goals, you find you are behind in getting updates to your mentor, and you haven't completed some the actions you were assigned. You feel bad about it, but don't know what to do as you are taxed for time.

Nevertheless, you feel that your mentor is a much larger part of the problem. Specifically:

1. You are upset that you have not had the chance to practice your public speaking yet in front of a large audience.
2. You are concerned that you are not meeting enough executives in order to build your network quickly.

3. You don't see the relevance of or have the time to read all the marketing reports, competitor reports, company background materials, annual reports and executive letters that your mentor has given you to help you learn more about the company – you are having trouble getting up to speed on your current job without having to learn all this unnecessary information.

4. You don't feel the executives you have met have shown much interest in meeting you – it feels to you like meeting people is a formality that no one really cares about.

5. Overall, you don't feel you have been getting enough of your mentor's attention – he/she appears preoccupied with other matters.

You want a more definite plan of action going forward to address these issues. That is your intention for this meeting.

How to Play This Role

- Begin the meeting with the usual pleasantries and thank the mentor for meeting with you, but you should display some sense of frustration and disappointment.

- If the mentor asks you to state your concerns and issues, start with a vague answer, stating that you are not happy with the relationship, or the opportunity that you have been provided, and you want more out of it.

- If the mentor asks you for further clarification start walking through the issues listed on the previous page. However, don't give all five at once . . . start with the first one or two, then wait for additional follow-up questions to elaborate on the other issues.

- If the mentor accepts some responsibility for the issues, become more open and willing to participate. If you feel the mentor is listening well and open to your position, then you can discuss the trouble you are having being a protégé while you are struggling in your job. Indicate your desire to move forward, but your lack of knowledge as to the best way to do so.

- If the mentor tries to put most or all of the responsibility/fault on you, continue to show frustration, gradually becoming more defensive over the course of the 15-minute meeting.

- At first, try to have the mentor develop the solutions in order to see if you can get the mentor to do most of the work. However, if the mentor continues to press for your ideas, gradually start offering some ideas.

- If the mentor shows a willingness to work collaboratively with you, then start to open up and offer some suggestions.

- If toward the end of the meeting you are not getting anywhere and no concrete actions have been set, start suggesting that it may be in the interest of both parties to end the relationship. Continue to show your frustration.

- If, at the end of the meeting, the mentor has (1) accepted some responsibility for the problems; (2) shown a commitment to work with you going forward; and (3) helped create a specific action plan, then state and show your excitement for moving forward.

Appendix J: Sample Wrap-up Activity

Purpose

To give participants an opportunity to reflect on what they have learned during the course and to identify specific actions they will take in order to make maximum use of the mentoring relationship.

Instructor Actions

1. At the end of the final topic, put up the Wrap-up Activity Slide and ask participants to answer the following questions by writing their comments on the supplied notepaper:

   - What are the top three things you learned during this program?
   - What three actions do you plan to take to make the most of your mentoring relationship?
   - What obstacles do you foresee to your full participation in the mentoring relationship?
   - What will you do to overcome these obstacles?

2. Separately for each question, ask participants to share some of what they noted. Note their answers on a flipchart.

3. For each question, the instructor should do the following:

   - For answers to question one, explain how the learning will help the participant in the mentoring relationship.
   - For answers to question two, ask the participant to elaborate on how that action will help him or her be an effective protégé or mentor.
   - For answers to question three, ask "why" these obstacles are apparent (this will help them identify ways to overcome them).
   - For answers to question four, encourage other participants to add their ideas for ways to overcome obstacles.

4. After everyone has had a chance to speak, summarize the information and thank the class.

Appendix K: Guidelines for Facilitating a Mentoring Agreement

The mentoring agreement is designed to facilitate an understanding between a mentor and a protégé as to the goals, boundaries, and roles of the relationship. Using the following guidelines, both the mentor and protégé should jointly discuss the talking points and reach agreement on each key issue. Record the applicable information in the attached document.

Step 1: Goals for the Relationship

- Discuss the desired outcomes of the mentoring relationship for the protégé and for the mentor.
- Form the goals using the SMART guidelines (i.e., Specific, Measurable, Achievable, Relevant, and Timely goals).

Step 2: Potential Barriers to Goal Achievement

- Discuss possible barriers or obstacles that may hinder achieving the goals just developed.
- Develop contingency plans to overcome these barriers or obstacles.

Step 3: Mentor's Role

- The protégé and mentor should discuss the primary function(s) that the mentor will provide. These could include serving as a role model, gaining the protégé visibility, providing psycho-social support, and/or preparing the protégé for a specific assignment or responsibility.

Step 4: Protégé's Role and Expectations

- The protégé and mentor should discuss the role of the protégé. Expectations surrounding communications, openness to learning, etc., are open for discussion.

Step 5: Confidentiality Parameters

- Discuss and agree on how sensitive information will be handled. Determine what information is confidential and what is not. To whom will non-confidential information be conveyed? The formal mentoring program's policies and guidelines should be consulted.

Step 6: Meeting Frequency, Communication Methods, and Location of Meetings

- Discuss and agree to the frequency of meetings between the protégé and mentor. The frequency of meetings will depend on the mentor's role, the goals of the relationship, and the structure of the mentoring program.
- The preferred method of meeting should be discussed and agreed to (e.g., face-to-face, telephone, or email).
- Discuss boundary conditions for phone calls.

Step 7: Length of the Relationship

- If not mandated by the organization, discuss and agree upon the approximate length of the relationship.

Step 8: Potential Conflicts and How to Overcome Them

- Discuss the types of issues that might bring the mentor and protégé into conflict (e.g., not devoting enough time for the relationship; not providing enough feedback).
- Discuss and agree to the steps that will take place should conflict occur. Multiple steps are preferred. Again, refer to the formal program's guidelines in developing these steps.

Mentoring Agreement Form	
Goals of the Mentoring Relationship • •	
Barriers to Reaching Goals • • •	**How Overcome?** • • •
Mentor's Role • • • •	**Protégé's Role and Expectations** • • • •
Confidentiality Standards	
Method of Communication • • •	**How Often for Each Method?** • • •
Length of Relationship	
Potential Conflicts • • •	**Steps to Resolve Conflicts** • • •

_____   _____

Mentor Signature   Date

_____   _____

Protégé Signature   Date

Sample Completed Form

Mentoring Agreement Form

Goals of the Mentoring Relationship

- To build the protégé's visibility and network with senior leaders
- To provide the protégé exposure to executive-level projects and work
- To enhance and broaden the protégé's leadership skills

Barriers to Reaching Goals	How Overcome?
<ul><li>Mentor will be out of the country for three months on an international assignment</li><li>Protégé is in final semester of EMBA program</li></ul>	<ul><li>Use company's video-conference system and emails to communicate</li><li>Program facilitator to help ensure protégé's meetings with executives take place</li><li>Protégé's supervisor to provide half-day each week to work on mentoring activities</li></ul>
Mentor's Role	**Protégé's Role**
<ul><li>Get protégé to participate on an executive-level committee</li><li>Provide specific and timely feedback supplemented with coaching and guidance</li><li>Have the protégé accompany to executive-level meetings and social events and introduce protégé to contacts</li><li>Arrange for opportunities to meet formally with executives</li><li>Provide protégé with training and reading materials</li></ul>	<ul><li>Attend all meeting and scheduled appointments</li><li>Keep mentor informed of all mentoring-related activities and outcomes</li><li>Seek additional opportunities to learn and develop</li><li>Participate fully in all scheduled and recommended activities, projects, etc.</li></ul>

Confidentiality Standards
Periodic feedback and development updates are to be provided to the mentoring steering committee. All other information is to be kept confidential as outlined in the program guidelines.

Method of Communication	*How Often for Each Method?*
<ul><li>Face-to-face meetings</li><li>Video-conferencing</li><li>Phone calls</li><li>Email</li></ul>	<ul><li>Monthly and as needed</li><li>Monthly and as needed</li><li>Weekly and as needed</li><li>As needed</li></ul>

Continued

Length of Relationship 1 year with potential to extend if desired.	
Potential Conflicts	*Steps to Resolve Conflicts*
• Given travel and work demands, main conflict would be real/perceived lack of effort and priority	• Each person should communicate their concerns timely and directly • Each person will generate one solution • Mentor and protégé will discuss and reach agreement on best solution • Refer to program facilitator if these steps are not successful

Appendix L: Career Planning Form

Name: Current Position:

Legacy I Want to Leave:
What Position and Level Do I Want To Achieve in My Career?:

Short-Term Career Goals (1–2 Years)	Mid-Term Career Goals (3–5 Years)	Long-Term Career Goals (8–10 Years)
Steps/Positions to Achieve Goal	**Steps/Positions to Achieve Goal**	**Steps/Positions to Achieve Goal**
• • •	• • •	• • •
What Needs Development?	**What Needs Development?**	**What Needs Development?**
• • •	• • •	• • •

Sample Career Planning Form

Name: Robin Public   Current Position: Engineer II

Legacy I Want to Leave: I want to be known as someone who had a positive impact on the lives of work colleagues at all levels of the organization, and who contributed significant growth to the business.

What Position and Level Do I Want To Achieve in My Career?
I would like to achieve a position at the Executive Vice-President level within the Engineering or Operations organization. Projected timeframe for this position would be 15–20 years.

Short-Term Career Goals (1–2 Years)	Mid-Term Career Goals (3–5 Years)	Long-Term Career Goals (8–10 Years)
To become Engineering Project Manager within the R&D Area (1 step up and lateral from current position).	To become Engineering Manager within the R&D Area (3 steps up from current position).	To become an Engineering Director within the Operations function (5 steps up from current position).
Steps/Positions to Achieve Goal	**Steps/Positions to Achieve Goal**	**Steps/Positions to Achieve Goal**
• Participate in the company's formal mentoring program. • Show excellent performance as an Engineer II. • Talk to people who have successfully progressed as Engineers to find out "what it takes."	• Excellent performance as an Engineering Project Manager. • Obtain and excel in mid-step position as Senior Project Manager. • Identify and secure a mentor from the Director level or higher, either through the formal program or informally.	• Strong track record of success in previous positions. • Obtain and excel in mid-step position as Engineering Manager in the Operations area. • Look for rotational assignments or cross-functional projects to build experience in other functional areas (e.g., Service & Repair; Sales & Marketing).

146

What Needs Development?	What Needs Development?	What Needs Development?
• Project management skills. • Lack of exposure and contacts at management levels. Need networking. • Interpersonal skills – communication and listening ability.	• Supervisory skills (e.g., performance management; coaching; delegation). • Finance and budget training. • Direct supervisory experience.	• Lack of exposure and contacts at executive levels of management. • Organizational savvy. • Executive presence and public speaking skills.

Appendix M: Mentoring Action Plan

Protégé: Mentor:
Date Created:

Developmental Area:	Developmental Objective:		
Actions	**Resources and Support Needed**	**Timeline**	**Criteria for Success**

GUIDELINES FOR COMPLETING THE MENTORING
ACTION PLAN

<u>Instructions</u>: The mentor and protégé can determine how best to complete the development form. Some mentor–protégé pairs find it beneficial to jointly complete the document. Others may find it best to have the protégé create a first draft, whereupon it is reviewed by the mentor then finalized in a joint planning session. However, it is not recommended that the mentor write the plan for the protégé.

Step 1: Select Developmental Area

- Considering the goals for the relationship, the protégé and mentor should select skill, knowledge, competency, or behavioral areas that would benefit from further development. Career goals, 360-degree feedback, performance appraisals, etc., can be used to guide these choices.

Step 2: Create a Developmental Objective

- For each target area, the mentor and protégé should develop a SMART goal that describes exactly what outcome is desired.
- Make the goal as behavioral in description as possible. For example, if a target area is "Communication Skills," one possible goal might be "To speak with fewer pauses and language fillers, to show more positive body language when speaking, and to use less hesitant language."

Step 3: Create Mentoring Actions

- The mentor and protégé should identify multiple, specific activities that the protégé will undertake to achieve the developmental goals. These activities should include a mix of formal (e.g., training; seminars; workshops) and informal (e.g., OJT; reading a book) learning methods, as well as a mix of passive (e.g., reading, training; observing a role model) and active (e.g., assignments; special projects; practice) practice methods.

Step 4: List Support Mechanisms

- The mentor and protégé should identify and list the support needed in order to implement the developmental activities. This could include other colleagues, time, or monetary resources.

Step 5: Timing and Milestones

- The mentor and protégé should jointly select the deadline for completing each developmental activity. An overall deadline for completing the target area's development may be set as well.
- For example, a mentor and protégé may allocate 12 months to significantly improve the protégé's communication skills. They may also set 3-, 6- and 9-month milestone dates to coincide with the completion of development activities and provide an opportunity to gauge progress.

Step 6: Criteria for Success

- The mentor and protégé should identify methods and criteria for measuring success. For example, to measure progress of "Communication Skills," success can be measured qualitatively through informal verbal feedback, and/or quantitatively through 360-degree feedback.

Sample Completed Form

Mentoring Action Plan

Protégé: Robin Public   Mentor: Jane Smith
Date Created: November, 2007

Developmental Area: Networking	Developmental Objective: To expand Robin's network and contact list outside of the engineering area, and to gain him more exposure and experience at the senior management level.		
Actions	**Resources and Support Needed**	**Timeline**	**Criteria for Success**
Robin will complete the "Network Mapping Exercise" in order to determine where his network is strong and where in the organization he is lacking contact.	Support from Robin's supervisor to grant time away from the job to meet new contacts and attend strategic planning meetings.	December, 2008	Within 6 months, a minimum of eight new members in Robin's network with whom he has regular and permanent contact.
Jane will introduce Robin to two manager(s) at his level from each of the Sales & Marketing, Manufacturing, Human Resources, Facilities, and Finance organizations.	Permission from the Senior Management Strategic Planning Committee to allow Robin to attend.	January– February, 2008	For each of the eight contacts, Robin is to have provided them with assistance on an issue of importance to them.

Continued

Robin will create a "contacts list" that contains the name, phone number, email address, and function/ role for each contact. In this spreadsheet Robin will also track the last time he met/ contacted the individual as well as applicable information that Robin will need in order to maintain the relationship (e.g., hobbies).	Time from the peer-level managers in other functions to meet and speak with Robin.	February, 2008	Completed contact spreadsheet with regular updates.
Robin will maintain regular contact with each person in his network; meeting/ phoning/emailing them a minimum of once per quarter, preferably more. Robin will also contact each person when he can provide him/her with help.	Support from HR in completing the "Network Mapping Exercise."	December– May, 2008	Number of times Robin has provided assistance; minimum of one per contact.
Jane will bring Robin to two Senior Management Strategic Planning Committee meetings over the next 6 months. She will introduce Robin to a minimum of two executives at each meeting.		December– May, 2008	Invited attendance to future Senior Management Strategic Planning Committee meetings.

Appendix N: Sample Reaction Form

Mentoring Relationship Reaction Form
Protégé Form

Instructions: Please complete the following survey by circling the appropriate response using the following scale:

1 = Strongly Disagree   2 = Disagree   3 = Agree   4 = Strongly Agree

1. The mentoring I received has helped me learn new skills.. 1 2 3 4
2. The mentoring I received has improved my performance 1 2 3 4
3. The mentoring I received has improved my commitment to this company 1 2 3 4
4. The mentoring I received has prepared me for broader responsibilities 1 2 3 4
5. The mentoring I received has helped broaden my network.................................. 1 2 3 4
6. The mentoring I received helped ease my adjustment into my new role 1 2 3 4
7. My mentor provided me with timely feedback..... 1 2 3 4
8. My mentor gave me frequent and constructive feedback and coaching.............. 1 2 3 4
9. The mentoring relationship has been a valuable use of my time 1 2 3 4
10. I am satisfied with the amount of mentoring I received.. 1 2 3 4
11. I am satisfied with the quality of mentoring I received.. 1 2 3 4

Comments

Please add any comments to further clarify your ratings.

Goal Attainment

In what ways have you developed, progressed, or improved as a result of your mentoring relationship?

Improvement Plans

Please note any changes you would like to see made to the mentoring program.

Appendix O: Sample Evaluation Plan

New Employee Socialization Mentoring Program

Purpose of Program: To orient, socialize, and rotate newly hired MBA graduates into entry-level management positions.

Goals of Program: To retain newly hired MBA graduates, to provide them experience in three different divisions, to build their network of contacts with employees and managers, and to orient them to the company's structure, culture, and policies.

Structure of Program: MBAs will be matched with a senior-level executive. The MBA and his or her mentor will meet at least once per month. Face-to-face monthly meetings are required, other meetings can take place via email, phone, face-to-face, etc. Both participants will attend a one-day orientation and skill-building session prior to starting the relationship. As part of the mentoring program, MBAs will rotate through 3 four-month assignments in different divisions of their choice.

Evaluation Plan

What is Measured?	How Measured?	When Measured?
Amount of learning that took place in training	• Paper and pencil test administered before and after training	Immediately following training
Reactions to training	• Questionnaire: open-ended comments • Questionnaire: ratings of satisfaction with training, usefulness of training, perceived benefit of training, and amount of learning participants believe took place	Immediately following training
Reactions to the mentoring program	• Interview: four questions gauging what is working, what is not working, what needs to change, and what support is needed	At the 6-month time interval
Number of MBAs who received performance ratings of 4 from all of their rotation supervisors	• HR Data Systems	Immediately after the mentoring relationship has ended
Strength of network	• Questionnaire: MBAs will indicate the number and names of their key contacts • Questionnaire: MBAs will numerically rate the strength of their network	Immediately following the mentoring relationship
Number of MBAs remaining employed	• HR Data Systems	Immediately following the mentoring relationship
Number of MBAs placed in positions of their top two choice	• HR Data Systems	Immediately following the mentoring relationship

Knowledge of the organization's structure and policies	• Paper and pencil test	Pre-test administered before the mentoring relationship begins and post-test administered after the mentoring relationship ends
Protégé & mentor participation	• Interview • Questionnaire: participants will rate the performance of their partner on six key competencies • Questionnaire: participants will indicate the degree to which they followed the program's structure	Immediately following the mentoring relationship

Sample Evaluation Plan

Global Sales Mentoring Program

Purpose of Program: To equip sales professionals with the knowledge, skills, and experience they will need in order to transfer from domestic to international accounts.

Goals of Program: To improve sales professionals' ability to influence and sell in multiple cultures, to build strong contacts with customers from the region he or she is assigned to, and to adapt to living in a new culture.

Structure of Program: Sales professionals will be paired with a senior sales executive currently in the region. The mentor will be at least two levels above the protégé. There are no requirements for the minimum number of meetings. The mentorship will last 6 months, beginning when the protégé physically moves to the new region. Both participants will attend a one-day orientation and skill-building session prior to starting the relationship.

Evaluation Plan

What is Measured?	How Measured?	When Measured?
Amount of learning that took place in training	• Paper and pencil test administered before and after training	Immediately following training
Reactions to training	• Questionnaire: open-ended comments • Questionnaire: ratings of satisfaction with training, usefulness of training, perceived benefit of training, and amount of learning participants believe took place	Immediately following training
Protégé satisfaction with new assignment	• Questionnaire: ratings of satisfaction with the new assignment and perceived fit within the new culture	Immediately after the mentoring relationship has ended

Protégé satisfaction with mentoring	• Questionnaire: ratings of satisfaction with the mentoring received	Immediately following the mentoring relationship
Mentor satisfaction with mentoring program	• Questionnaire: ratings of satisfaction with the program	Immediately following the mentoring relationship
Sales performance	• US Dollar amount of sales	Three months after the relationship has ended
Number of new customers obtained	• Sales & Marketing Data Systems	Three months after the relationship has ended

• Results will be compared to a control group of sales professionals who received a similar international assignment and all the required training EXCEPT formal mentoring.

Notes

1 Introduction

1 Kram (1985).
2 Allen, Eby, Poteet, Lentz, and Lima (2004).
3 Eby and Allen (2008); Eby, Rhodes, and Allen (2007).
4 Hung (2003).
5 Underhill (2006).
6 See, for example, Allen et al. (2004); Allen and O'Brien (2006); Eby, Allen, Evans, Ng, and DuBois (2008); Underhill (2006).
7 Egan and Song (2008).
8 Dubois, Holloway, Valentine, and Cooper (2002).

2 Planning and Providing Infrastructure

1 See, for example, Goldstein and Ford (2002); Noe (2004).
2 Rhoades and Eisenberger (2002).
3 Rynes and Rosen (1995).
4 Milne, Blum and Roman (1994).
5 Ibid.
6 Koberg, Boss, and Goodman (1998).
7 Parise and Forret (2008).
8 Eddy, Tannenbaum, Alliger, D'Abate, and Givens (2001).
9 Piper and Piper (2000).
10 Eby and Lockwood (2005).
11 Hegstad and Wentling (2004).
12 Allen, Poteet, and Burroughs (1997); Hegstad and Wentling (2005).

3 Participant Recruitment and Selection

1 Eddy, Tannenbaum, Alliger, D'Abate, and Givens (2001).
2 Baldwin, Magjuka, and Loher (1991); Klimoski and Hicks (1987).
3 Allen, Eby, and Lentz (2006a); Ragins, Cotton, and Miller (2000).
4 Allen, Eby, and Lentz (2006b).
5 Parise and Forret (2008).
6 Ragins, Cotton, and Miller (2000).
7 Eddy et al. (2001).
8 Ibid.
9 Noe (1988).
10 Wanberg, Kammeyer-Mueller, and Marchese (2006).
11 See Turban and Lee (2007) for a review.
12 Colquitt, LePine, and Noe (2000).
13 Allen, Poteet and Burroughs (1997).
14 See, for example, Fields (2002); Lester and Bishop (2000).
15 Allen et al. (1997).
16 See Allen (2007) for a review.
17 Allen (2003).
18 Gentry, Weber, and Sadri (2008).
19 Allen et al. (1997).
20 Ragins et al. (2000).
21 Allen, Poteet, and Russell (2000).
22 Grube and Piliavin (2000).
23 Matthews (2003).
24 Eddy et al. (2001).
25 Allen and Poteet (1999); Smith, Howard, and Harrington (2005).
26 Allen (2003); Messmer (2001).
27 Wanberg et al. (2006).
28 Allen and Eby (2008); Allen, Eby, and Lentz (2006a).

4 Matching Mentors and Protégés

1 Eby and Lockwood (2005).
2 Mullan (1984).
3 Hamon and Ingoldsby (2003).
4 Eddy, Tannenbaum, Alliger, D'Abate, and Givens (2001).
5 Ragins, Cotton, and Miller (2000).
6 Parise and Forret (2008).
7 Allen, Eby, and Lentz (2006a).
8 Viator (1999).
9 Parise and Forret (2008).

10 See, for example, Cotton, Vollrath, Froggatt, Lengnick-Hall, and Jennings (1988); Leana, Locke, and Schweiger (1990); Wagner (1994).
11 Tesluk, Vance, and Mathieu (1999).
12 Sagie and Aycan (2003).
13 Chao, Walz, and Gardner (1992); Eddy et al. (2001).
14 Meikle, Poteat, Rodopman, Shockley, Yang, and Allen (2007).
15 Hall (2003); Miller (2007).
16 Meikle et al. (2007).
17 Tracy, Jagsi, DPhil, and Tarbell (2004).
18 Allen and Eby (2003); Ensher and Murphy (1997); Turban, Dougherty, and Lee (2002).
19 Eby, Butts, Lockwood, and Simon (2004); Eby and Lockwood (2005); Eby and McManus (2004).
20 Bercheid and Regan (2005).
21 Acitelli, Douvan, and Veroff (1993); Allen and Eby (2003).
22 See Hale (2000) for a thorough discussion of issues related to matching on the basis of similarity versus dissimilarity.
23 Eddy et al. (2001).
24 Brown, Zablah, and Bellenger (2008).
25 Allen, Day, and Lentz (2005).
26 Blake-Beard (2001).
27 Allen, Eby, and Lentz (2006a).
28 Ragins et al. (2000).
29 Ibid.
30 Allen, Eby, and Lentz (2006a).
31 Eby and Lockwood (2005).
32 Allen, Eby, and Lentz (2006a).
33 Grove, Zald, Lebow, Snitz, and Nelson (2000).

5 Training

1 See, for example, Noe (2004); Goldstein and Ford (2002).
2 Allen, Eby, and Lentz (2006a).
3 Allen, Eby, and Lentz (2006b).
4 Parise and Forret (2008).
5 Sipe and Roder (1999).
6 Parise and Forret (2008).
7 Noe (2004); Goldstein and Ford (2002).
8 Gray (1988).
9 See Eby (2007) for a review of negative experiences in mentoring relationships.
10 Allen, Eby, and Lentz (2006b).

11 DuBois, Holloway, Valentine, and Cooper (2002).
12 Eby and Lockwood (2005).
13 Noe (2004); Goldstein and Ford (2002).

6 Mentoring Structures and Processes

1 Viator (1999).
2 Latham (2007).
3 Bercheid and Regan (2005).
4 Johnson and Ridley (2004).
5 Eddy, Tannenbaum, Alliger, D'Abate, and Givens (2001).
6 Ragins, Cotton, and Miller (2000).
7 Viator (1999).
8 Grossman and Rhodes (2002); Miller (2007); Sipe (1996).
9 Allen, Eby, and Lentz (2006b); Orpen (1997); Meikle, Poteat, Rodopman, Shockley, Yang, and Allen (2007).
10 Meikle et al. (2007).
11 Eddy et al. (2001).
12 Mendleson, Barnes, and Horn (1989).
13 Allen and Eby (2003).
14 Catalyst (1993); Forret, Turban, and Dougherty (1996); Eddy et al. (2001).
15 Grossman and Rhodes (2002); Miller (2007); Sipe (1996).
16 Kram (1985).
17 Morrow and Styles (1995).
18 Styles and Morrow (1992).

7 Monitoring and Program Evaluation

1 Wanberg, Welsh, and Hezlett (2003).
2 Egan and Song (2008).
3 Eby, Lockwood and Butts (2006).
4 Kirkpatrick (1975, 1994).

References

Acitelli, L. K., Douvan, E., & Veroff, J. (1993). Perceptions of conflict in the first year of marriage: How important are similarity and understanding? *Journal of Social and Personal Relationships, 10,* 5–19.

Allen, T. D. (2003). Mentoring others: A dispositional and motivational approach. *Journal of Vocational Behavior, 62,* 134–54.

Allen, T. D. (2007). Mentoring relationships from the perspective of the mentor. In B. R. Ragins & K. E. Kram (Eds). *The handbook of mentoring at work: Theory, research, and practice* (pp. 123–47). Thousand Oaks, CA: Sage Publications.

Allen, T. D., Day, R., & Lentz, E. (2005). The role of interpersonal comfort in mentoring relationships. *Journal of Career Development, 31,* 155–69.

Allen, T. D. & Eby, L. T. (2003). Relationship effectiveness for mentors: Factors associated with learning and quality. *Journal of Management, 29,* 469–86.

Allen, T. D., & Eby, L. T. (2008). Mentor commitment in formal mentoring relationships. *Journal of Vocational Behavior, 61,* 309–16.

Allen, T. D., Eby, L. T., & Lentz, E. (2006a). The relationship between formal mentoring program characteristics and perceived program effectiveness. *Personnel Psychology, 59,* 125–53.

Allen, T. D., Eby, L. T., & Lentz, E. (2006b). Mentorship behaviors and mentorship quality associated with formal mentoring programs: Closing the gap between research and practice. *Journal of Applied Psychology, 91,* 567–78.

Allen, T. D., Eby, L. T., Poteet, M. L., Lentz, E., & Lima, L. (2004). Career benefits associated with mentoring for protégés: A meta-analysis. *Journal of Applied Psychology, 89,* 127–36.

Allen, T. D., & O'Brien, K. (2006). Formal mentoring programs and organizational attraction. *Human Resource Development Quarterly, 17,* 43–58.

Allen, T. D., & Poteet, M. L. (1999). Developing effective mentoring relationships: Strategies from the mentor's viewpoint. *The Career Development Quarterly, 48,* 59–73.

Allen, T. D., Poteet, M. L., & Burroughs, S. M. (1997). The mentor's perspective: A qualitative inquiry and agenda for future research. *Journal of Vocational Behavior, 51,* 70–89.

Allen, T. D., Poteet, M. L., & Russell, J. E. A. (2000). Protégé selection by mentors: What makes the difference? *Journal of Organizational Behavior, 21,* 271–82.

Baldwin, T. T., Magjuka, R. J., & Loher, B. T. (1991). The perils of participation: Effects of choice of training on trainee motivation and learning. *Personnel Psychology, 44,* 51–65.

Bercheid, E., & Regan, P. (2005). *The psychology of interpersonal relationships.* New Jersey: Pearson Prentice Hall.

Blake-Beard, S. D. (2001). Taking a hard look at formal mentoring programs: A consideration of potential challenges facing women. *Journal of Management Development, 20,* 331–45.

Brown, B. P., Zablah, A. R., & Bellenger, D. N. (2008). The role of mentoring in promoting organizational commitment among black managers: An evaluation of the indirect effects of racial similarity and shared racial perspectives. *Journal of Business Research, 61,* 732–38.

Catalyst (1993). *Mentoring: A guide to corporate programs and practices.* New York: Catalyst.

Chao, G. T., Walz, P. M., & Gardner, P. D. (1992). Formal and informal mentorships: Comparison on mentoring functions and contrast with nonmentored counterparts. *Personnel Psychology, 45,* 619–36.

Colquitt, J. A., LePine, J. A., & Noe, R. A. (2000). Toward an integrative theory of training motivation: A meta-analytic path analysis of 20 years of research. *Journal of Applied Psychology, 85,* 678–707.

Cotton, J., Vollrath, D. A., Froggatt, K. L., Lengnick-Hall, M. L., & Jennings, K. R. (1988). Employee participation: Diverse forms and different outcomes. *Academy of Management Review, 13,* 8–22.

DuBois, D. L., Holloway, B. E., Valentine, J. C., & Cooper, H. (2002). Effectiveness of mentoring programs for youth: A meta-analytic review. *American Journal of Community Psychology, 30,* 157–97.

Eby L. T. (2007). Understanding relational problems in mentoring: A review and proposed investment model. *The handbook of mentoring at work: Theory, research, and practice* (pp. 323–44). Thousand Oaks, CA: Sage Publications.

Eby, L. T., & Allen, T. D. (2008). Moving toward an interdisciplinary dialogue in mentoring scholarship. *Journal of Vocational Behavior, 72,* 159–67.

Eby, L. T., Allen, T. D., Evans, S. C., Ng, T., & DuBois, D. (2008). Does mentoring matter? A multidisciplinary meta-analysis comparing mentored and nonmentored individuals. *Journal of Vocational Behavior, 72,* 254–67.

Eby, L. T., Butts, M., Lockwood, A., & Simon, S. (2004). Protégés' negative mentoring experiences: Construct development and nomological validation. *Personnel Psychology, 57*, 411–47.

Eby, L. T., & Lockwood A. (2005). Protégés' and mentors' reactions to participating in formal mentoring programs: A qualitative investigation. *Journal of Vocational Behavior, 67*, 441–58.

Eby, L. T., Lockwood, A., & Butts, M. (2006). Organizational support for mentoring: A multiple perspectives approach. *Journal of Vocational Behavior, 68*, 267–91.

Eby, L. T., & McManus, S. E. (2004). The protégé's role in negative mentoring experiences. *Journal of Vocational Behavior, 65*, 255–75.

Eby, L. T., Rhodes, J., & Allen, T. D. (2007). Definition and evolution of mentoring. In T. D. Allen & L. T. Eby (Eds). *Blackwell handbook of mentoring: A multiple perspectives approach* (pp. 7–20). Oxford: Blackwell.

Eddy, E., Tannenbaum, S., Alliger, G., D'Abate, C., & Givens, S. (2001). Mentoring in industry: The top 10 issues when building and supporting a mentoring program. Technical report prepared for the Naval Air Warfare Training Systems Division (Contract No. N61339–99-D-0012), Orlando, FL.

Egan, T. M., & Song, Z. (2008). Are facilitated mentoring programs beneficial? A randomized experimental field study. *Journal of Vocational Behavior, 61*, 351–62.

Ensher, E. A., & Murphy S. E. (1997). Effects of race, gender, and perceived similarity, and contact on mentor relationships. *Journal of Vocational Behavior, 50*, 460–81.

Fields, D. L. (2002). *Taking the measure of work: A guide to validated scales for organizational research and diagnosis*. Thousand Oaks, CA: Sage Publications.

Forret, M. L., Turban, D. B., & Dougherty, T. W. (1996). Issues facing organizations when implementing formal mentoring programmes. *Leadership & Organization Development Journal, 17*, 27–30.

Gentry, W. A., Weber, T. J., & Sadri, G. (2008). Examining career-related mentoring and managerial performance across cultures: A multilevel analysis. *Journal of Vocational Behavior. 72*, 241–53.

Goldstein, I. L., & Ford, J. K. (2002). *Training in organizations: Needs assessment, development, and evaluation* (4th ed.). Belmont, CA: Wadsworth/Thomson Learning.

Gray, W. A. (1988). Developing a planned mentoring program to facilitate career development. *Career Planning and Adult Development Journal, 4*, 9–16.

Grossman, J. B. & Rhodes, J. E. (2002). The test of time: Predictors and effects of duration in youth mentoring programs. *American Journal of Community Psychology, 30*, 199–219.

Grove, W. M., Zald, D. H., Lebow, B. S., Snitz, B. E., & Nelson, C. (2000). Clinical versus mechanical prediction: A meta-analysis. *Psychological Assessment, 12,* 19–30.

Grube, J. A., & Piliavin, J. A. (2000). Role identity, organizational experiences, and volunteer performance. *Personality and Social Psychology Bulletin, 26,* 1108–20.

Hale, R. (2000). To match or mis-match? The dynamics of mentoring as a route to personal and organisational learning. *Career Development International, 5,* 223–34.

Hall, J. C. (2003). *Mentoring and young people: A literature review.* SCRE Research Report 114. Glasgow: University of Glasgow.

Hamon, R. R., & Ingoldsby, B. B. (2003). *Mate selection across cultures.* Thousand Oaks, CA: Sage Publications.

Hegstad, C. D., & Wentling, R. M. (2004). The development and maintenance of exemplary formal mentoring programs in Fortune 500 companies. *Human Resource Development Quarterly, 15,* 421–48.

Hegstad, C. D., & Wentling, R. M. (2005). Organizational antecedents and moderators that impact on the effectiveness of exemplary formal mentoring programs in Fortune 500 Companies in the United States. *Human Resource Development International, 8,* 467–87.

Hung, V. (2003). Mentorship memo: A time-honoured learning style is taking on new guises in the 21st century, but there are still some basic rules to following any mentor–mentee relationships. Make sure you understand them. *CMA Management, 77,* 10–1.

Johnson, W. B., & Ridley, C. M. (2004). *The elements of mentoring.* New York: Palgrave-Macmillan.

Kirkpatrick, D. (1975). *Techniques for evaluating training programs.* Alexandria, VA: ASTD.

Kirkpatrick, D. (1994). *Evaluating training programs: The four levels.* San Francisco, CA: Berrett-Koehler.

Klimoski, R. J., & Hicks, W. D. (1987). *Academy of Management Journal, 30,* 542–52.

Koberg, C. S., Boss, R. W., & Goodman, E. (1998). Factors and outcomes associated with mentoring among health-care professionals. *Journal of Vocational Behavior, 53,* 58–72.

Kram, K. E. (1985). *Mentoring at work: Developmental relationships in organizational life.* Glenview, IL: Scott Foresman.

Latham, G. P. (2007). *Work motivation: History, theory, research and practice.* Thousand Oaks, CA: Sage.

Leana, C. R., Locke, E. A., & Schweiger, D. M. (1990). Fact and fiction in analyzing research on participative decision making: A critique of Cotton, Vollrath, Froggatt, Lengnick-Hall, and Jennings. *Academy of Management Review, 15,* 137–46.

Lester, P. E., & Bishop, L. K. (2000). *Handbook of tests and measurement in education and the social sciences*, 2nd ed. Lanham, MD: The Scarecrow Press, Inc.

Matthews, B. A. (2003). Enhancing the protective capacity of mentoring relationships: Strengthening the social bond. Unpublished doctoral dissertation. University of Cincinnati.

Meikle, H., Poteat, L., Rodopman, O. B., Shockley, K. M., Yang, L., & Allen, T. D. (2007). *Evaluation of the CAS formal mentoring program*. Tampa, FL: The University of South Florida.

Mendleson, J. L., Barnes, A. K., & Horn, G. (1989). The guiding light to corporate culture. *Personnel Administrator, 34*, 70–2.

Messmer, M. (2001). *Human resources kit for dummies*. New York: Wiley Publishing, Inc.

Miller, A. (2007). Best practices in formal youth mentoring. In T. D. Allen, & L. T. Eby (Eds). *Blackwell handbook of mentoring: A multiple perspectives approach*. Oxford: Blackwell.

Milne, S. H., Blum, T. C., & Roman, P. M. (1994). Factors influence employees' propensity to use an employee assistance program. *Personnel Psychology, 47*, 123–45.

Morrow, K. V., & Styles, M. B. (1995). *Building relationships with youth in program settings: A study of Big Brothers/Big Sisters*. Philadelphia: Public/Private Ventures.

Mullan, B. (1984). *The mating trade*. London: Routledge & Kegan Paul.

Noe, R. A. (1988). An investigation of the determinants of successful assigned mentoring relationships. *Personnel Psychology, 41*, 457–79.

Noe, R. A. (2004). *Employee training and development*. Boston: McGraw-Hill/Irwin Professional.

Orpen, C. (1997). The effects of formal mentoring on employee work motivation, organizational commitment, and job performance. *Learning Organization, 4*, 53–60.

Parise, M. R., & Forret, M. (2008). Formal mentoring programs: The relationship of program design and support to mentors' perceptions of benefits and costs. *Journal of Vocational Behavior, 72*, 225–40.

Piper, H., & Piper, J. (2000). Disaffected young people as the problem: Mentoring as the solution. Education and work as the goal. *Journal of Education and Work, 13*, 77–94.

Ragins, B. R., Cotton, J. L., & Miller, J. S. (2000). Marginal mentoring: The effects of type of mentor, quality of relationship, and program design on work and career attitudes. *Academy of Management Journal, 43*, 1177–94.

Rhoades, L., & Eisenberger, R. (2002). Perceived organizational support: A review of the literature. *Journal of Applied Psychology, 87*, 698–714.

Rynes, S., & Rosen, B. (1995). A field survey of factors affecting the adoption and perceived success of diversity training. *Personnel Psychology, 48*, 247–70.

Sagie, A., & Aycan, Z. (2003). A cross-cultural analysis of participative decision-making in organizations. *Human Relations, 56,* 453–73.

Sipe, C. L. (1996). *Mentoring: A synthesis of P/PV's research: 1988–1995.* Philadelphia: Public/Private Ventures.

Sipe, C. L., & Roder, A. E. (1999). *Mentoring school-age children: A classification of programs.* Philadelphia: Public/Private Ventures.

Smith, W. J., Howard, J. T., & Harrington, K. V. (2005). Essential formal mentor characteristics and functions in governmental and non-governmental organizations from the program administrator's and the mentor's perspective. *Public Personnel Management, 34,* 31–50.

Styles, M. B., & Morrow, K. V. (1992). *Understanding how youth and elders form relationships: A study of four linking lifetimes programs.* Philadelphia: Public/Private Ventures.

Tesluk, P. E., Vance, R. J., & Mathieu, J. E. (1999). Examining employee involvement in the context of participative work environments. *Group and Organization Management, 24,* 271–99.

Tracy, E. E., Jagsi, R., DPhil, R. S., & Tarbell, N. J. (2004). Outcomes of a pilot faculty mentoring program. *American Journal of Obstetrics and Gynecology, 191,* 1846–50.

Turban, D. B., Dougherty, T. W., & Lee, F. K. (2002). Gender, race, and perceived similarity effects in developmental relationships: The moderating role of relationship duration. *Journal of Vocational Behavior, 61,* 240–62.

Turban, D. B., & Lee, F. K. (2007). The role of personality in mentoring relationships: Formation, dynamics, and outcomes. *The handbook of mentoring at work: Theory, research, and practice* (pp. 21–50). Thousand Oaks, CA: Sage Publications.

Underhill, C. M. (2006). The effectiveness of mentoring programs in corporate settings: A meta-analytical review of the literature. *Journal of Vocational Behavior, 68,* 292–307.

Viator, R. E. (1999). An analysis of formal mentoring programs and perceived barriers to obtaining a mentor at large public accounting firms. *Accounting Horizons, 13,* 37–53.

Wagner, J. A. (1994). Participation's effect on performance and satisfaction: A reconsideration of research evidence. *Academy of Management Review, 19,* 312–20.

Wanberg, C. R., Kammeyer-Mueller, J., & Marchese, M. (2006). Mentor and protégé predictors and outcomes of mentoring in a formal mentoring program. *Journal of Vocational Behavior, 69,* 410–23.

Wanberg, C. R., Welsh, E. T., & Hezlett, S. A. (2003). Mentoring research: A review and dynamic process model. *Research in Personnel and Human Resources Management, 22,* 39–124.

Author Index

Authors not mentioned in the text have an "n" number after the page reference. More details will be found on pages 165–8

Subject Index

9 781405 179898